# Spanish
*Cocina Casera Española*
# Home Cooking

*Text and photographs by Miriam Kelen*

Cocina Casera, Inc., Minneapolis, 2002

*Derechos reservados ©Museu Diocesà de Tarragona. 14c. altarpiece. Maldà. Lleida*

Text and photographs Copyright ©2002 by Miriam Kelen

Library of Congress Cataloging-in-Publication Data available.

ISBN 0-9715115-0-0

Book Design and Prop Styling by Emily Oberg
Food Styling by Audrey Nelson, Judy Tills
Photography by Miriam Kelen
Production by Leslie Hacking
Pre Press and Printing by Pettit Network, Inc., Afton, MN

Printed in Hong Kong

10 9 8 7 6 5 4 3 2 1

Cocina Casera, Inc., 1921 Humboldt Ave. So., Minneapolis, MN 55403
www.cocinacasera.com

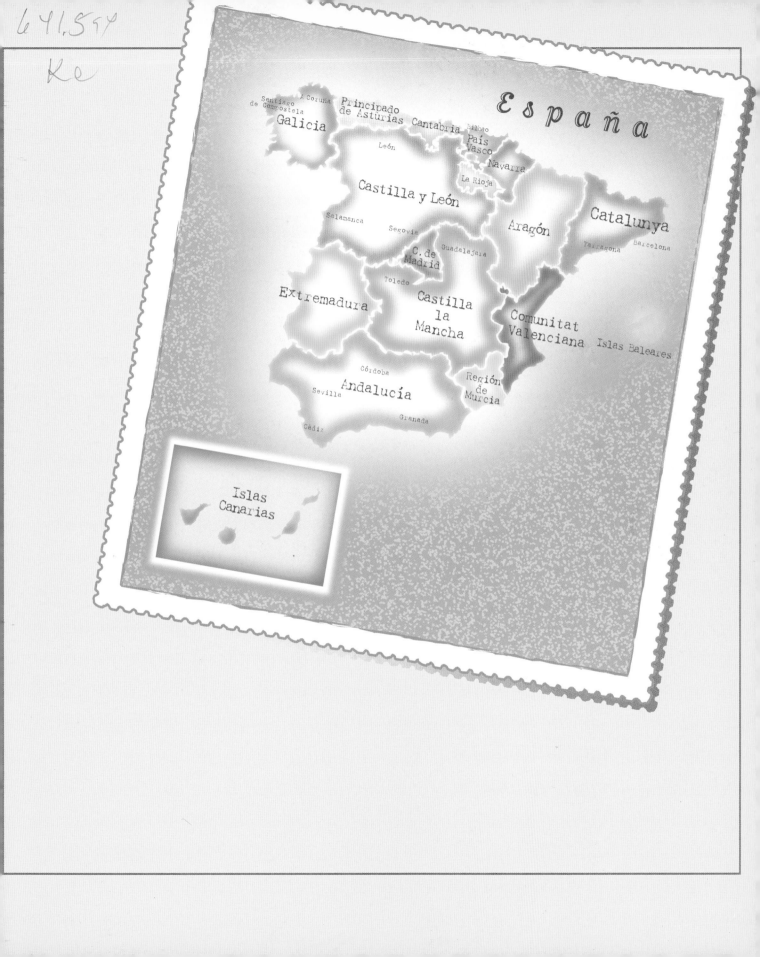

# A dedication

To Nacho...

who first suggested collecting
recipes and writing a book of
home cooking. It was to be
written as if it were just for
him and me, except that it would
sell millions of copies.

Dear friend and muse, thank you.

# Contents

*Doorway, Sevilla*

# How it all began

Without going back to my high school Spanish class, where I believe we learned one song, or to the endless hours I spent studying government language cassettes for my travels to Mexico in the '70s, the journey to this book began with an invitation to celebrate a wedding in Spain in 1994. As my husband and I traveled through the country, I realized how much I loved the culture, the language, the food, the beauty of the countryside, and the openness and generosity of the people.

As it happened, that period coincided with my entry into the Internet, and on a whim I put my name on a list, looking for people with whom to exchange letters in Spanish. I ended up making some amazing and enduring friendships. It was on line, during a discussion of recipes, that Nacho from Barcelona suggested we get together and write a cookbook. It seemed like a perfectly natural idea. Though we had no idea where such a book would lead, neither did we doubt that it would yield an array of delicious discoveries.

The original idea was to introduce people to real Spanish home cooking, the kinds of traditional foods that moms fix with love, that grandmothers know best, that sisters-in-law are famous for, that men concoct when they have the time. Nacho lined up the first group of cooks, and through other pen pals, families of people I knew in Minneapolis, and friends from the wedding, the list of cooks grew and grew. Coincidence and destiny also played a part; I met and was able to interview a number of chefs, some of international renown.

*Celebrating food and friendship*

In all, I made several long trips to Spain, camera and tape recorder in hand, learning as I went. I was invited to share many home-cooked meals, from whole-family gatherings to dinner for two—always in good company. People generously gave me recipes and helpful explanations as well. And at bars, in restaurants, wherever I was, I asked for more ideas.

One spring day, on my quest for the best gazpacho, a waiter in Córdoba said to me, "You Americans always ask how things are made so you can go home and do the same thing." "Of course," I answered, "that's the idea!"

Now it's your turn to enjoy.

# Acknowledgements

This book is as much about friendship as it is about cooking, as much about navigating the Internet as crisscrossing Spain in search of recipes. For all of us participants, the project was a great leap of faith, yet it turned out to be one of the great joys of my life. To all my cooks and hosts who showed me the true meaning of the word welcome, an enormous thank you. This never would have come true without you.

The organizers, however, deserve special mention.

**Nacho Jiménez Uroz** not only inspired me with the original idea, but he organized friends and family throughout Barcelona to show me the delights of Catalan cuisine.

**Manuel Jiménez de León** drove me to every beautiful corner and microclimate of Tenerife in the Canary Islands; his wonderful family welcomed me at their table every day of my stay.

**Carmen Borrás Tortosa** and her friends in Valencia were sophisticated and enthusiastic eaters, if not cooks; it fell to her mother to explain paella.

**Sabina Montoya Vilar**, my first cook, saw me at my most disorganized when I shot endless pictures without film in the camera. Fortunately, she and her sister, Ceferina, came to the rescue with more superb home cooking.

**Nuria Jiménez Uroz** gave me a home away from home for almost two months on my first visit. Our many late nights of food, wine, conversation and chocolate were all and always the best. And to the rest of the Jiménez family—Isabel, Pepe, and Sara, I thank you for hospitality and friendship.

**Idoia Marqués Celaya** took me home to her family in Basque Country where eating well is a serious proposition. She, herself, makes perhaps the best Tortilla de Patata in Spain.

**Ellanor Ravenga** hosted me and organized fabulous meals in both her home in Madrid and her country house, an old mill, near Segovia.

**Mercé Casanovas**, her father Manuel, and her mother Josefina Pagès invited me to a family birthday party practically my first day in Barcelona; I have returned to their home for many elaborate and sumptuous meals.

**Eduard Torrell**, one of my first Internet friends, wouldn't enter the kitchen, but his mother, Maria, and sister, Monica, joined in with enthusiasm. And I got to visit his home town of Riudoms and nearby Tarragona.

Thanks, finally, to **Isabel Pérez** who, from a chance meeting, has become a dear friend. Though she didn't contribute recipes, she arranged a fascinating meeting with her friend, **Ferran Adrià**. Even though this was to be a book about home cooking, when the opportunity arose to spend time with some of the most distinguished and congenial chefs in Spain, I jumped. After all, as many of them said, even the most far-out dish has flavors in the familiar.

*Sant Narcís. Girona*

7

*Enjoying horchata and fartons at Daniel's, Valencia*

My travels took me to many different parts of Spain, but this is by no means a complete culinary tour. It's about the cooking in homes, and sometimes restaurants, I visited around the country. The brief descriptions of regions I did go to came from, where else? the Internet. It seemed fitting.

Many traditional and regional specialties are, of course, included in the collection. But recipes don't always stay within neat geographical borders. As gifts from mothers, grandmothers, in-laws and friends, they get packed up with other treasured possessions and moved from place to place. In their new homes, ingredients might change to reflect local produce, meats or cheeses. Or, seasonings might take on a regional accent. Preparation can also vary from the traditional, as hand blenders, pressure cookers, and freezers add new convenience. Translating the recipes to U.S. measures and available ingredients, and in some cases tastes, has brought about modifications, too.

Of course, some recipes never change, from generation to generation to generation—nor should they. And there is one bond that is common throughout all Spain: a passion for good food and a love of good company with whom to share it.

Minneapolis,
May, 2002

*"The Gypsy" Cave, Sacromonte, Granada (opposite)*

# Galicia

The land of two seas—Galicia—has four provinces: A Coruña, Pontevedra, Ourense, and Lugo.

Galicia has a long tradition of culinary artistry, which is surely part of its great appeal to visitors. Seafood, fish, meat, game, fruits, vegetables, wine, cheese—the quality and bounty of Galicia's fields, orchards and waters are well known, as is the expert hand with which it is all prepared. With so much variety and abundance, it's difficult to say which Galician dishes are most typical. Two of the better known are Lacón con Grelos, pork shoulder cooked with turnip greens to which cachelos (potatoes) and chorizo are added; and **Caldo Gallego**, a rich winter-time soup made with meats, potatoes, beans and turnip greens. Summer in Galicia is time for dark green **Pimientos de Padrón,** little peppers, fried and sprinkled with coarse salt. They are often served with the waiter's warning: "Careful, there might be some hot ones in there!"

For fish and seafood lovers, Galicia is truly paradise. Fish include freshwater trout, salmon, eel, shad and lamprey and, from the sea, hake, cod, sole, turbot, grouper and sea bass. As for shellfish, the breathtaking array is Spain's best: shrimp, clams, mussels, scallops, lobster, crayfish, spider crab, sea crab, prawns, cockles, razor clams, oysters, and goose barnacles (which are found in very few places in the world). And, starring at every fair throughout Galicia is the local favorite, **Pulpo a la Gallega**—octopus, cooked, sliced and sprinkled with olive oil, coarse salt and paprika. It is typically served on a round wooden plate and speared with toothpicks.

Vieiras (scallops) are featured in many bars and restaurants. For centuries, the scallop shell has been the symbol of pilgrims going to Santiago de Compostela. Vieiras a la Gallega are scallops baked in the shell, with a mixture of chopped onions, parsley and bread crumbs on top.

Another specialty is **Empanada Gallega,** a delicious filled pastry characterized by its fine, light crust. The filling can be just about anything—fish, seafood, meat, vegetables—and is seasoned with saffron, oil, peppers and onions. Empanada Gallega is found all over Spain, but should definitely be tried in Galicia.

*Tarta de Santiago*

Popular Galician cheeses include soft, creamy Tetilla, semi-hard San Simón, Arzúa-Ulloa with a buttery, yogurty flavor, and Cebreiro which is shaped like a chef's hat.

Galicia's five Denominación de Origen wines are: Ribeiro, Valdeorras, Rías Baixas, Monterrei, and Ribeira Sacra. In reds, look for an elegant, aromatic Mencía; in whites, a subtle Godello or, to accompany fish and seafood, a light, fruity Albariño. Albariño vines were originally brought to Galicia by monks from the Rhine and Moselle valleys.

If you want to indulge in a typical Galician dessert, there are Melindres, honey fritters; **Filloas**, tender custard-filled crepes; or the almond-rich, melt-in-your-mouth Tarta de Santiago to try. And for your grand finale, **Queimada**—the flaming "witch's brew" made with orujo, a clear liquor distilled from the skins and seeds of grapes. With the proper incantation, Queimada is said to chase the evil spirits away.

*Fishing boats. A Coruña*

# Caldo Gallego

## Hearty Galician Bean Soup

*Pilar Rodriguez Goyanes*

"I learned to cook a little from my aunt. My mother died very young. I also worked in a restaurant in A Coruña, and it's there that I learned about seafood. I'm from the interior, from Lugo, where it's more meat, vegetables, and all that. I like to cook and always believed I could. I cook with a little imagination and never do anything literally."

| | |
|---|---|
| *2 cups dried white beans* | *1 lb. small potatoes, peeled, halved* |
| *8 cups water* | *2 to 3 whole chorizos* |
| *2 oz. salt pork* | *1 lb. turnip or collard greens, thick stems* |
| *1 (1/4-lb.) slice of ham, cut into pieces* | *removed, coarsely chopped* |
| *2 teaspoons salt* | *Salt and freshly ground pepper* |

1. Soak beans overnight in water to cover. Drain just before using.
2. Bring 8 cups water to a boil in large soup pot or Dutch oven. Add drained beans, salt pork, ham pieces and 2 teaspoons salt. Return to a boil; skim off foam. Reduce heat; cover and simmer 45 minutes.
3. Add potatoes and chorizos; simmer 20 minutes.
4. Add greens; simmer an additional 10 minutes or until potatoes and greens are tender. Season to taste with salt and pepper. Just before serving, slice chorizos.

8 servings

As a chef explained it to me, grelos are the leaves of the turnip, picked when flowering. The greens blend well with cooked pork which needs an acid green. It makes it lighter, easier to digest.

# Cordero al Horno

## Marinated Roast Lamb

| | |
|---|---|
| 5 garlic cloves, peeled | Freshly ground pepper |
| 1/4 cup chopped fresh parsley | 1 large onion, sliced |
| 1 teaspoon salt | 1 cup water |
| 1/4 cup olive oil | 8 medium baking potatoes, peeled, |
| 1 (3-lb.) boneless leg of lamb | halved or quartered |

1. In food processor or with mortar and pestle, process garlic, parsley and salt until fine. Stir in oil. Spread mixture over lamb. Season to taste with pepper. Cover; refrigerate several hours or overnight to marinate.
2. Heat oven to 350°F. Cover bottom of roasting pan with onion slices. Top with lamb. Arrange potatoes around lamb. Pour 1 cup water over potatoes.
3. Roast 45 to 60 minutes or until lamb reaches desired doneness. (Roast 12 to 20 minutes per pound, depending on desired doneness. Meat thermometer should reach 140°F. for rare, 155°F. for medium.)

6 to 8 servings

In Galicia, a fundamental part of many meals is 'cochelos,' which are potatoes, peeled and cut into uniform slices and boiled in water and salt. Or, they can be roasted. Galicia is very rich in food and, perhaps because of the cold climate, there's also a tendency to eat heartier meals.

# Consomé con Huevos

## Consommé with Swirled Eggs

*Mari Carmen Valcarcel Sánchez*

"I learned to cook as I went along. When you get married you think, 'let's try this, let's try something else.' Galician food for me is special and one of the most delicious. In the north the cooking is always more flavorful. The raw materials are very good, produce as well as dairy products ... and the fish! You'll see when you go there. In Galicia they eat well."

| | |
|---|---|
| *1 ham bone or smoked ham shank* | *1 medium tomato* |
| *1 lb. beef bones* | *2 sprigs fresh parsley* |
| *1 to 1 1/2 lb. chicken wings* | *1 bay leaf* |
| *1 to 2 leeks* | *2 teaspoons salt* |
| *1 medium onion* | *8 to 10 cups water* |
| *1 medium carrot* | *8 eggs, beaten, if desired* |

1. Place all ingredients except water and eggs in large soup pot or Dutch oven; add enough of the water to cover. Bring to a boil; skim off foam. Reduce heat; cover and simmer about 2 hours.
2. Remove ham bone, beef bones and chicken wings from soup pot. Strain broth into another container; cool. When cooled, skim off fat. (The broth can be prepared a day ahead.)
3. Just before serving, bring broth to a boil. Pour into individual cups or bowls. Stir 1 beaten egg into each serving. This will turn consommé into a creamy soup.

8 servings

Loved the velvety eggs against the smoky consomme.

*Taster*

# Conejo Orensano

## Rabbit, Orense Style

| | |
|---|---|
| 1 (3 to 3 1/2-lb.) rabbit, cut into serving pieces | 1 medium carrot, coarsely chopped |
| 2 tablespoons olive oil | 1/2 cup milk |
| Salt and freshly ground pepper | 1 tablespoon flour |
| 1 small onion, chopped | 1/2 cup dry white wine |
| | 1/2 teaspoon paprika |

1. Wash rabbit; pat dry. Heat oil in large skillet over medium-high heat until hot. Add rabbit pieces; cook until all sides are well browned, adding salt and pepper to taste. When almost browned, add onion and carrot to cook with rabbit.
2. In small bowl, blend milk and flour; stir in wine and paprika. Push rabbit pieces to sides of skillet. Add milk mixture; bring to a boil, stirring constantly.
3. Rearrange rabbit pieces around skillet. Reduce heat; cover and simmer about 1 hour or until rabbit is tender, turning occasionally. Add extra water if sauce cooks off too quickly.

4 to 6 servings

In my village they began to eat at 3 o'clock in the afternoon, and it got to be 7 o'clock and they were still sitting there eating. What nonsense. Now it happens a little less.

# *Filloas*

## Custard-Filled Crepes

| **Filling** | **Crepes** |
|---|---|
| 1 1/2 cups whole milk | 1 cup whole milk |
| 1/2 cup sugar | 2 whole eggs |
| 2 tablespoons cornstarch | 1 egg white |
| 2 egg yolks, beaten | 3/4 cup flour |
| 1 teaspoon vanilla | 1/4 teaspoon salt |
| | Butter |

1. To make custard, heat 1 1/2 cups milk in medium saucepan over medium heat. Combine sugar and cornstarch; stir into milk as it is heating. Gradually stir in 2 egg yolks, cooking until mixture is thickened, stirring constantly.
2. Remove saucepan from heat. Stir in vanilla. Cool. (If desired, custard can be made ahead and refrigerated.) Serve at room temperature.
3. To make crepes, in medium bowl, combine 1 cup milk, eggs, egg white, flour and salt; mix until smooth. For easier handling, let stand 30 minutes before cooking.
4. Heat small skillet over medium heat until hot. For each crepe, lightly coat skillet with butter. Spoon 2 tablespoons batter into hot skillet; tilt quickly to cover bottom. When crepe has set, turn and cook about 1 minute or until other side is set. (Crepes can be made ahead; stack between sheets of waxed paper until ready to use.)
5. To serve, spread 1 tablespoon filling on each crepe; roll up.

14 to 16 filled crepes

Filloas is a word in Gallego. The crepes can be filled with pastry cream; they can be filled with salty things, too, like spinach. With honey they're also very good. This is a typical dessert, above all during Lent.

Hórreo, for storing grain

Galicia is green, very green and lush. And
dotting the countryside everywhere are hórreos,
the granaries on stilts, where grain was
traditionally stored. My contacts in Galicia
came through Lareira, a restaurant association,
and they were most helpful. In Santiago, I met
the owner of several restaurants who, in
addition to lots of information, gave me a taste
of the best-quality ham, made from pigs that
range free and eat only acorns, and some "tit"
cheese, very mellow and soft. In Vigo, Europe's
biggest fish port, my host had a country inn
where we feasted on salt cod and smoked salmon
salad, pulpo a la gallega, fish croquettes the
size of oval marbles, empanada squares, country
bread and then ... the main course. For dessert,
we sampled flan, egg yolk tart, chocolate
truffles and apple tarts. All with lots of
Albariño wine and a fine Portuguese port to
finish. In Coruña, at dawn, I went to the
fish market. The boats came in with crates of
fish on ice, enough to fill a whole warehouse.
With no room left to move between the crates,
the fishermen walked all over them in their
rubber boots. Wash that fish!

España
POR AVION

# Lenguado con Vieiras y Endibia

## Fillet of Sole with Scallops and Endive

*José Manuel Villasenín Aldonza*
*Ruta Jacobea, Santiago de Compostela*

"The essential parts of Galician cuisine are seafood and fish, although there are good meats as well. Galicia is a region where, thank God, we have everything. I believe all of Spain comes here to eat shellfish. ...I still like to cook from time to time, but I've gotten out of the kitchen. The truth is, a business with 140 employees takes time away from my being able to be in the kitchen. I miss it because I have it inside me."

| | |
|---|---|
| 2 (12-oz.) sole or flounder fillets | 3/4 cup dry white wine |
| 8 medium to large scallops | 2 large heads Belgian endive, julienned |
| 1 tablespoon olive oil | (about 3/4 cup) |
| 1 teaspoon butter | 3/4 cup whipping cream |
| Salt | |

1. Rinse sole fillets and scallops; pat dry. Cut each fillet lengthwise into 4 long strips. Wrap each strip around 1 scallop; secure with toothpick.
2. Heat oil and butter in large skillet over medium heat until butter melts. Add fish and scallop rolls; cook about 1 minute on each side, lightly seasoning each side with salt.
3. Add wine; bring to a boil. Reduce heat to low; cover and simmer 5 minutes or until fish flakes easily with fork and scallops are opaque. Remove rolls from skillet; place on serving platter. Cover to keep warm.
4. To make sauce, strain liquid from skillet; pour liquid back into cleaned skillet. Bring to a boil. Add endive and cream; return to a boil. Simmer, uncovered, 2 to 3 minutes to thicken sauce. Serve sauce over fish and scallop rolls.

4 servings

Traditional food like this can be presented very well. You eat more amply and you pay less than with 'designer cuisine,' where one eats with the eyes. But it, too, has a market and is making its way. You have to have something for everyone.

Cocinero COOK

# *Bacalao Daurado*

## Golden Cod Scramble

*José Carlos Lemos Domínguez*
*Las Bridas Restaurante, Vigo; Pousada del Castillo de Soutomaior*

"In my restaurant, our philosophy of cooking is that it's what the customer wants. And when customers get tired of something, then we look for new ideas. We introduce something new every day. Our menu is in the Galician tradition with some Portuguese influence. Sometimes I go into the kitchen. I like it, but then something's missing in the dining room ... leaving the customers alone."

| | |
|---|---|
| *1/4 lb. dried boneless salt cod* | *6 eggs* |
| *3 to 4 tablespoons olive oil* | *Chopped fresh parsley* |
| *2 medium red potatoes, shredded* | *Black olives (such as kalamata)* |
| *1 garlic clove, peeled* | |

1. Shred salt cod coarsely by hand; rinse thoroughly under cold running water for 5 to 8 minutes. Drain well; set aside.*
2. Heat 2 tablespoons of the oil in large nonstick skillet over medium heat until hot. Add shredded potatoes; fry until golden brown, stirring frequently. Remove potatoes from skillet; place on paper towels to drain.
3. Add remaining 1 to 2 tablespoons oil to skillet; heat until hot. Add garlic; cook until browned. Remove garlic from skillet. Add cod; sauté several minutes to heat.
4. Beat eggs in large bowl. Stir in fried potatoes. Add to skillet; cook over medium heat until eggs are set but not dry, stirring frequently. Sprinkle with parsley. Serve with olives.

4 to 5 servings
*Place the rinsed cod in a towel and twist to remove the water.

I began cooking when I was 12, when I emigrated to Portugal. Portuguese cooking is similar because it's basic pot cooking, slow cooking. There's a lot of French influence, too. After the Second World War, in the great restaurants in Lisbon, there were French chefs and Italian chefs. Many came to work because, since Portugal didn't intervene in the war, it was very comfortable to live there. Bacalao Daurado is a Portuguese recipe.

Cocinero
COOK

# Ensalada de Bacalao y Salmón

## Cod and Smoked Salmon Salad

*1/4 lb. dried boneless salt cod*
*1 head lettuce*
*1 (3-oz.) pkg. smoked salmon (lox)*
*Extra virgin olive oil*
*1 garlic clove, thinly sliced, if desired*

1. Cover salt cod with cold water; refrigerate 24 hours, changing water 4 times.
2. Drain cod. Press with paper towels to remove excess moisture. Remove and discard skin and membranes. Cut cod into 1/4-inch-thick pieces.
3. Arrange lettuce leaves on individual salad plates. Top each with sliced cod and smoked salmon, cut into pieces. Drizzle generously with oil. Garnish with garlic.

4 to 6 servings

I'd like to write a cookbook, but I don't have time. I had a weekly radio show talking about cooking, and listeners called to ask for recipes and ways to prepare things. Now I have a program, 10 minutes, no more, about cooking economically.

Spanish wines have enjoyed a long history. In fact, production has been certified for thousands of years: the art of viticulture was introduced by the Romans. Today, Spain is one of the leading producers in the world, with over 100 different classes of wine. To guarantee the quality and control of Spanish wines, the Instituto Nacional de Denominaciones de Origen (INDO) issues an official catalog. Currently it lists up to 60 wine-making districts which either have excellent physical and climatic conditions or produce particularly good wines. To understand a little better what you're buying, if it says Cosecha, the wine is young and has never been aged in an oak barrel. Crianza wines have been aged in oak for six months to a year and aged in the bottle for two years. Reserva has been in oak for two years, Gran Reserva for even longer.

Among the most widely exported wines are Rioja, Ribera del Duero, Penedès and La Mancha. Also, sherry (vino de Jerez), a fortified wine from Andalucía, and cava, Spain's sparkling wine made by the champagne method, which comes primarily from the Penedès region of Catalunya.

Spanish beer is of the lager type, and is usually served well chilled. It is especially popular in tapas bars.

Spirits and liqueurs worth a mention are the Andalusian brandies, aguardiente (eau de vie, 80% alcohol), Galician orujo (distilled from grape skins and seeds), anís (anise flavored liqueur), and, from Basque Country, patxaran de endrinas (sloe liqueur) and sidra (apple cider).

*José María Ramos*
*Director, Pousada del Castillo*
*de Soutomaior*

*"The wine culture has evolved a lot in Spain. Ten years ago we Spanish didn't understand wine. Now we understand it well and value a good wine.*

*In the last 10-15 years, in bars, in homes, in restaurants, people have become accustomed to drinking wines from grapes that are chosen and professionally prepared. In Spain we have very good natural products like grapes, but before, the winemaking was done at home by artisans and the wine had a lot of acidity. They used chemical products without controls and didn't let the grapes mature in the right conditions. Today, because of the regulations of the Denominación de Origen, it's all changed. For example, the Albariño from Galicia: the managers can't harvest whenever they choose. They're obligated to harvest the grapes when they have the necessary level of sugar."*

*Ruth Lozano Rodriguez*
*Consejo Regulador Ycoden Daute Isora, Tenerife*

*"The flavor of wine depends on where the vines are cultivated. If it's near the sea, there's more sodium. If it's 50 meters or 150 meters from the sea, there's a different taste. In the old days we exported sweet wine from the Canary Islands. We're trying to reclaim this tradition, recovering parcels of land, making cultivation more profitable. We're exporting more and more to the United States. It's a very important market because there are people in the U.S. who know a lot about wine; they're not people we have to educate."*

*Homemade spirits: Market, Santiago de Compostela (opposite)*

# Menestra de Verduras

## Seasonal Vegetable Medley

*Rosa María Míguez Vásquez*
*El Gallo de Oro, Arteixo*

"I eat at the restaurant every day. There are some dishes I try at home and then pass on to the restaurant, but normally I don't cook there. I'm not, let's say, at the stove. I only supervise, and cook at home. At home it depends on my mood, and the time, and the ingredients there are in the pantry. But I'm not afraid of preparing anything—not meat, fish, vegetables or pastry!"

| | |
|---|---|
| *2 tablespoons olive oil* | *Water* |
| *1 medium tomato, chopped* | *Salt* |
| *1 medium leek, sliced* | *1/4 lb. fresh green beans* |
| *2 garlic cloves, chopped* | *1 cup frozen peas* |
| *4 medium carrots, halved crosswise* | *White or red wine vinegar, if desired* |
| *1/2 head cauliflower, broken into florets* | |

1. Heat oil in large saucepan over medium heat until hot. Add tomato, leek and garlic; sauté until softened.
2. Add carrots and cauliflower; barely cover vegetables with water. Add salt to taste. Bring to a boil. Reduce heat; cover and simmer 10 minutes.
3. Add green beans; simmer 5 minutes. Add peas; simmer a few minutes or until all vegetables are tender. Drain. Just before serving, sprinkle with vinegar.

4 to 6 servings

Menestra is made with different types of vegetables that are cooked very slowly. We prepare it with a little garlic; afterward we add a little vinegar. (Some people don't add the vinegar.) It depends on the season, but Menestra can be made with Brussels sprouts, chard, spinach, leeks or peas. It is a first course, eaten alone.

# Salpicón de Mariscos

## Marinated Seafood Salad

| | |
|---|---|
| 1/2 lb. small or medium cooked shrimp, shelled* | 1/4 cup extra virgin olive oil |
| 1 small onion, finely chopped | 1 to 2 hard-cooked eggs, peeled, chopped |
| 1 medium red bell pepper, coarsely chopped | Juice of 1/2 lemon |
| | Salt and freshly ground pepper |

1. In serving bowl, combine shrimp, onion and bell pepper. Drizzle with oil. Cover; refrigerate at least 1 hour before serving.
2. Just before serving, sprinkle with eggs and lemon juice. Season to taste with salt and pepper.

*The original version was made with lobster and crab which are more plentiful in Galicia, but the salad is delicious with any seafood combination.

4 servings

Ours is traditional cooking, but always with innovations because we have a regular clientele. We have four or five different menus according to the season. Everything we make is with top-quality natural ingredients.

Cocinero
COOK

## Percebes

Sweet and succulent, "the percebe is," as a waiter holding a basket full of them once proudly proclaimed to me, "the king of shellfish."

*José Manuel
Villasenín Aldonza*

*Percebes, goose barnacles*

*"The percebe is a shellfish unique to Galicia. Well, in the north of Africa there are percebes but they're different, much larger and not as black. They've stopped gathering percebes along the whole coast at one time. Now the zones are surveyed and for one year they can fish in a certain zone, in the following year, a different one. It's very well controlled.*

*There are percebes practically the whole year, but if the sea is very rough, it's not possible to get them. In fact, every year in Galicia people die gathering percebes. I don't know, 8, 10, 12 people. The sea dashes them against the rocks. The percebes are on the rocky cliffs—very dangerous. But the people have to live on something, no? The fishermen put themselves in a lot of danger, not only with the percebes, in everything. The seas in Galicia are the seas ..."*

## Sepia or Chocos

In the U.S., 'sepia' and 'chocos' are known as cuttlefish, which is a cephalopod mollusk related to the squid. It is not often available, even in specialty fish markets, though you might be able to locate frozen cuttlefish in Asian markets. The recipes in this book, however, work equally well with squid, which can be found in most supermarkets and co-ops. Cuttlefish is rounder and generally meatier; squid is longer.

*Fish market, Madrid*

*Fresh from Galician waters (opposite)*

# País Vasco

Basque Country is made up of the provinces of Alava, Vizcaya and Gipúzcoa. It's a dreamy looking place, green from the rain, chilly, with low-hanging clouds and lots of cyclists out on the hills.

Basque cooking inspires a passion that has been passed down in family kitchens as well as in the uniquely-Basque gastronomic societies, or txokos. These private clubs take cooking and eating very seriously. Though traditionally for men only, today many people have txokos at home or in a place they share with friends, both men and women. They gather to cook, be social and taste the meal. If you're ever lucky enough to be invited, don't miss the chance to go! You'll discover that Basque Country is an eater's paradise.

Basque cuisine remained practically unchanged until the 1970s when young chefs began to combine the traditional and the "nouvelle." By trying different ingredients, flavor and texture combinations, and original ways of preparation, they made Basque cooking a creative and exciting mix. Dishes like Crab-filled Pancakes, Eel Salad, Leek Loaf in Pastry, **Stuffed Peppers**, and Cheesecake with Bilberries soon took their place on Basque menus.

In general, in Basque Country, the sea has been a better provider than the land. Its stars are merluza (hake), and bacalao (salt cod), found in the ever-popular Merluza en Salsa Verde (hake in green sauce), **Bacalao a la Vizcayna** (cod with a sauce of dried peppers and onions), and Bacalao al Pil-Pil, in which salt cod is shaken in hot oil until its gelatin is released and makes a sauce.

Other Basque sea dishes to try are **Marmitako**, a fisherman's stew made with tuna; **Txipirones en Su Tinta**, squid in its own ink; and angulas, baby eels which are quickly dipped in boiling oil with garlic, hot pepper and salt, and eaten with a wooden fork. The price of these little eels is now so high that they are often "made" out of fish and sold frozen.

Ocean fish are not the only Basque specialties. There are outstanding dishes made with Pyrenees beef, flavorful lamb, or the long spicy pork sausages known as txistorra. In Basque Country, the killing of the pig is still celebrated in rural areas with a party called a txerriboda. The damp climate is not suitable for curing pork, however, so it's usually eaten fresh or salted.

Finally, in Basque Country there is a great variety of game: boar, deer, hare, pigeon, woodcock, quail and partridge. And from the woods, in spring and fall, an extensive variety of mushrooms to grill, bake or scramble with eggs.

As in other parts of Spain, there is a Basque tradition of the txikiteo, going from bar to bar to drink small amounts of wine and enjoy pintxos—little sandwiches, or pieces of cheese, tortilla, meat, fish or vegetables on toothpicks. The bill is tallied by the number of toothpicks on your plate.

The best known cheese from Basque Country, where shepherding has always played an important role, is Idiazabal, an exquisite raw milk variety from native Latxa sheep. Idiazabal is soft and creamy when young, sharper and more aromatic when mature. Roncal is another Basque cheese worth discovering, as is the goat's-milk cheese from Vizcaya. Mamia (sheep's milk curds), is a true Basque dessert. It was originally prepared in wooden barrels over hot coals, the origin of its burnt taste.

From Basque vineyards, best known is the Rioja Alavesa, which has earned an international reputation. Reds from Basque Country are made from tempranillo and garnacha grapes, whites from the viura. The young, fruity-flavored wine, Txakolí, is ideal with fish

*Fishing port of Bermeo (opposite)*

and seafood. From Basque orchards, sidra (cider) is extremely popular. Produced for centuries in farmhouses, sidra is a combination of sweet and tart apples which gives it a special sweet-sour taste and a lovely straw color. Sidra is typically served at 13° to 15°C. (55° to 59° F.), and kept in dark bottles to protect it from the light. Like Txakoli, it is poured from a height of 30 to 40 centimeters (11-3/4 to 15-3/4 inches) to release the complex flavors as it hits the glass. It is said that sidra should never remain too long in the glass!

Patxaran, a superb after dinner drink made from the wild sloe plum, also comes from Basque Country. Once just a local homemade drink, it is now esteemed throughout Spain.

*Museo Guggenheim, Bilbao*

# *Pudin de Bonito*

## Baked Tuna Pudding

*Carmen Ruiz*

"In Basque Country, and also for my family, mealtime is very important. It's social ... for eating, talking, discussing, laughing. In our house, whoever is seated at our table becomes part of the family."

| | |
|---|---|
| 3 (6-oz.) cans tuna, drained* | 1/4 teaspoon pepper |
| 1/2 cup whipping cream or half-and-half | 3 eggs, separated |
| 1 to 2 tablespoons tomato paste | Mayonnaise |
| 1 teaspoon extra virgin olive oil | Capers, if desired |
| 1 teaspoon red wine vinegar | |

1. Heat oven to 350°F. Grease and flour 8x4-inch loaf pan.** In large bowl, combine tuna, cream, tomato paste, oil, vinegar, pepper and egg yolks; mix well.
2. In small bowl, beat egg whites until soft peaks form. Fold into tuna mixture. Pour into loaf pan. Place pan in larger pan of water.
3. Bake 35 to 40 minutes or until knife inserted in center comes out clean. Cool slightly.
4. Invert pudding onto serving plate. Garnish with mayonnaise; sprinkle with capers. Serve warm or cold.

*Use high-quality tuna packed in water.

**For easier removal, line pan with foil; grease and flour foil.

8 servings

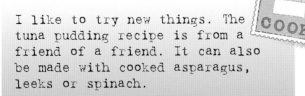

I like to try new things. The tuna pudding recipe is from a friend of a friend. It can also be made with cooked asparagus, leeks or spinach.

# Pimientos Rellenos

## Stuffed Peppers

*Mari Carmen Marqués*

"We spent a year in Girona where the food is nothing like what we have here. They use more spices. When I travel, I like to try things, to investigate—what do they have there? But I find that spices can take away the flavor of the food. Each thing should taste like what it is."

### Peppers
1 (7.5 to 8-oz.) jar piquillo peppers

### Filling
2 tablespoons olive oil

2 tablespoons chopped onion

3 tablespoons flour

1/2 teaspoon salt

3/4 cup chicken broth

1/4 cup dry white wine*

1 cup shredded cooked fish
  (such as cod, monkfish or tuna)**

Olive oil for frying

1 egg, beaten

Flour

1. Drain peppers on paper towels.
2. Heat 2 tablespoons oil in medium saucepan over medium heat until hot. Add onion; sauté until light golden brown. Stir in flour and salt; cook until mixture bubbles for 1 minute. Gradually add chicken broth and wine. Bring to a boil. Reduce heat; simmer until bubbly and thickened. Reserve 1/4 cup sauce. Stir fish into remaining sauce.
3. Stuff peppers with fish mixture.
4. Heat 3/4 inch of oil in large skillet over high heat until very hot. Dip stuffed peppers in egg; coat with flour. Add to skillet; fry, about 4 at a time, until a golden-brown crust forms on each side of pepper. Drain on paper towels; place on serving platter. Serve with reserved sauce.

*An additional 1/4 cup chicken broth can be used in place of the wine.

**About 3/4 lb. uncooked fish will make 1 cup shredded cooked fish.

6 servings

You can make the béchamel with crayfish, or hake, or monkfish. It takes time to fill all the peppers with a spoon, but it's not difficult.

COOK

# *Langostinos a la Plancha*

## Sautéed Prawns with Parsley Sauce

**Sauce**

2 tablespoons chopped fresh parsley

2 to 3 garlic cloves, chopped

Juice from 1 or 2 lemons (about 1/4 cup)

1 tablespoon water

1 teaspoon salt

1 lb. prawns or jumbo shrimp in shells

1 tablespoon olive oil

1. In food processor or with mortar and pestle, process parsley and garlic. Add lemon juice, water and salt; mix well.

2. Rinse prawns; pat dry. Heat oil in large paella pan or skillet over medium-high heat until hot. Add prawns; cook and stir 2 to 3 minutes or until prawns turn pink. Gradually stir in sauce as prawns cook.

3 to 4 servings

I'm someone who likes to try things. But our husbands, when it's mealtime, they're more traditional.

# Macedonia de Frutas

## Fruit Macédoine

| | |
|---|---|
| *1 (15-oz.) can peach halves or slices in heavy syrup* | *2 kiwi fruits, peeled, sliced* |
| | *1 teaspoon sugar* |
| *1 (8-oz.) can pineapple chunks in unsweetened juice* | *1/4 cup orange-flavored liqueur (such as Cointreau)* |
| *1 cup seedless green or red grapes* | *1 tablespoon rum* |
| *2 oranges, peeled, sliced* | *2 bananas, sliced* |

1. In medium bowl, combine canned fruits and juices with grapes, oranges and kiwi fruits.
2. Sprinkle with sugar; pour on orange-flavored liqueur and rum.
3. Just before serving, add banana slices; stir gently.

4 to 6 servings

Macedonia is delicious with any kind of fruit and any liqueur; your choice!

*Mercat de la Boqueria, Barcelona*

Many Spanish recipes call for tomatoes to be peeled, seeded and chopped. This can be done quickly by immersing the tomatoes in boiling water for about 10 seconds. Peel, from the stem end; halve crosswise; carefully squeeze out and discard the seeds and juice. Chop as directed in the recipe.

If the dish doesn't require pieces of tomato, the pulp can easily be extracted by halving the tomato crosswise and grating it, over a plate, with the large holes of a grater. In Spain, you can also find plastic containers with a grater lid. There are approximately three medium or two large tomatoes to a pound.

# Tortilla de Patata

## Traditional Potato Omelet

*Idoia Marqués Celaya*

"In the bars (in Basque Country there are a lot of them), eating 'pintxos' (tapas) is a tradition. They put them out to accompany the drinks, usually wine. There have always been groups of friends who meet every midday and late afternoon to go to the neighborhood bars. The custom is to have small glasses of wine or beer so there's time to get to all the bars. That's the story!"

3/4 to 1 cup safflower or sunflower oil

4 medium baking potatoes, peeled, cut into 1/2-inch cubes

1 medium onion, chopped

1 1/4 teaspoons salt

5 eggs

1. Heat oil in large nonstick skillet over medium heat until hot. Add potatoes and onion; sprinkle with 1 teaspoon of the salt. (Oil should cover potatoes.) Cook without stirring about 15 minutes or until potatoes are tender but not brown. Drain potatoes and onion in colander, reserving 2 tablespoons oil.*
2. In medium bowl, lightly beat eggs with remaining 1/4 teaspoon salt. Add potatoes and onion; stir well to coat with egg mixture.
3. Heat reserved 2 tablespoons oil in skillet over high heat until hot. Pour egg mixture into skillet; move skillet back and forth over burner to cook evenly. Reduce heat to medium-high; cook about 3 minutes or until bottom is browned, loosening edges with spoon if mixture sticks to sides of skillet.
4. Cover skillet with plate or large lid; invert skillet so omelet flips onto plate. Slide omelet back into skillet to cook other side. Repeat until both sides are golden and omelet is still juicy inside.
5. Cut omelet into wedges. Serve warm or at room temperature.

*Cool and strain remaining oil and save for frying.

4 main-dish servings or 8 to 10 appetizer servings

I learned this from my mother. It's easy and quick. With practice I now have my own way of making it. ...
If you want to add peppers, put them in after the potatoes because they cook more quickly.

# *Pollo a la Cerveza*

## Chicken in Beer Sauce

| | |
|---|---|
| 2 tablespoons olive oil | 2 garlic cloves, finely chopped |
| 1/4 cup flour | 2 large carrots, chopped |
| 2 teaspoons salt | 1 medium green bell pepper, chopped |
| 1/4 teaspoon pepper | 2 medium tomatoes, peeled, chopped* |
| 3 to 3 1/2 lb. cut-up chicken | 1 (12-oz.) bottle beer |
| Olive oil | 2 medium baking potatoes, peeled, cut |
| 1 large onion, chopped | into 1/2-inch cubes |

1. In large resealable plastic bag, combine flour, 1 teaspoon of the salt and the pepper. Add chicken pieces; seal bag and toss to coat.
2. Heat oil in large skillet over medium-high heat until hot. Add chicken; cook 20 to 25 minutes or until browned. Remove chicken from skillet.
3. Reduce heat to medium; if necessary, add additional oil. Add onion and garlic to same skillet; cook about 3 minutes or until onion is transparent.
4. Add carrots and bell pepper; cook 3 minutes. Add tomatoes and remaining 1 teaspoon salt; cook 5 minutes, stirring occasionally.
5. Stir in beer and potatoes. Transfer mixture to large saucepot or Dutch oven. Top with chicken. Bring to a boil. Reduce heat to low; cover and simmer 30 minutes.
6. Uncover saucepot; cook 10 minutes or until chicken is fork-tender and juices run clear.

*See page 35.

4 servings

Nice combination, don't change a thing.

# Bacalao con Pimientos Rojos

## Salt Cod with Roasted Red Peppers

*Miren Celaya*

"When I got married I didn't have any idea how to cook. I fixed some eggs because my mother always did. I chose what she had made. When I decided to cook something, I called one of my sisters and asked her, 'how did we make that? How is it made?' so I would be well informed."

---

*1 lb. dried boneless salt cod*

*1 (13-oz.) jar roasted red bell peppers, drained*

*1/3 cup olive oil*

*4 garlic cloves, peeled*

**Salt**

---

1. Cover salt cod with cold water; refrigerate 24 hours, changing water 4 times.
2. Drain cod. Press with paper towels to remove excess moisture. Remove and discard skin and membranes. Cut cod into 4 pieces. Set aside.
3. Cut roasted peppers in half, then into thin strips. Set aside.
4. Heat oil in large skillet or cazuela (a wide, shallow earthenware casserole) over medium heat until hot. Add garlic; cook until browned. Remove and discard garlic.
5. Add cod and roasted peppers to skillet; cook 7 to 9 minutes or until fish flakes easily with fork. Sprinkle with salt.

4 servings

When the garlic cloves are browned, I remove them. They're there to give flavor to the oil. It you like more garlic, add more. ... I put the roasted peppers on top and a little between the pieces of fish, but carefully, so as not to break the slices. One way or another, bacalao is delicious!

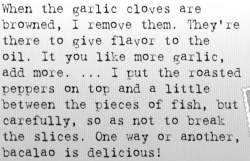

# Bacalao a la Vizcayna

## Basque-Style Cod

| | |
|---|---|
| 1 1/2 lb. dried boneless salt cod* | 2 to 3 medium onions, chopped |
| 4 dried chiles (such as Spanish ñoras or New Mexico style) | 1 medium carrot, chopped |
| | 1 medium green bell pepper, chopped |
| 2 tablespoons olive oil | 2 garlic cloves, chopped |
| 2 (3/8-inch-thick) slices day-old white bread, halved | 1 teaspoon tomato paste, if desired |
| | 1/2 teaspoon salt |
| 1 cup water | Freshly ground pepper |

1. If using salt cod, cover cod with cold water; refrigerate 24 hours, changing water 4 times.
2. Soak dried chiles in hot water for 45 minutes or until flesh can be scraped out with a spoon. Drain; remove seeds, scrape out flesh and discard skin. Set aside.
3. Heat oven to 350°F. Drain salt cod. Press with paper towels to remove excess moisture. Remove and discard skin and membranes. Set aside.
4. Heat oil in large skillet over medium-high heat until hot. Add bread slices; sauté until golden brown on both sides. Remove bread from skillet; place in small bowl. Add 1 cup water to bowl; soak bread until softened.
5. In same skillet, over medium heat, combine onions, carrot, bell pepper and garlic; sauté until softened. Lightly squeeze bread to remove water; add to skillet with flesh from dried chiles, tomato paste, salt and pepper. Cool slightly. In food processor or blender, process mixture until it forms a thick sauce.
6. Lightly oil large baking dish. Arrange cod in dish; top with sauce.
7. Bake 15 to 20 minutes or until thoroughly heated and fish flakes easily with fork.

*Fresh cod can be substituted for the salt cod.

6 servings

Instead of using paprika, we use the 'meat' of dried peppers to add flavor and color.

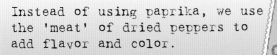

# Marmitako

## Fishermen's Stew

| | |
|---|---|
| *2 dried chiles (such as Spanish ñoras or New Mexico style)* | *4 medium red potatoes, peeled, cut into bite-sized pieces* |
| *2 tablespoons olive oil* | *4 cups fish broth\*\** |
| *1 medium onion, chopped* | *1/2 to 1 teaspoon salt* |
| *2 medium tomatoes, peeled, diced\** | *1 lb. fresh tuna* |
| *1 medium green bell pepper, chopped* | *Salt and freshly ground pepper* |
| *2 garlic cloves, chopped* | |

1. Soak dried chiles in hot water for 45 minutes or until flesh can be scraped out with a spoon. Drain; remove seeds, scrape out flesh and discard skin. Set aside.
2. Heat oil in large saucepan over medium heat until hot. Add onion; sauté until softened. Add tomatoes, bell pepper, garlic and flesh from dried chiles; sauté until softened.
3. Add potatoes, fish broth and salt. Bring to a boil. Reduce heat; cover and simmer 15 to 20 minutes or until potatoes are almost tender.
4. Rinse tuna; cut into bite-sized pieces. Add to stew; cover and simmer until tuna turns white. Season to taste with salt and pepper.

\*See page 35.

\*\*Fish broth can be purchased at specialty fish markets. Or, use a combination of bottled clam broth and water, or the recipe for fish broth from Bocinegro Canario, page 207.

4 servings

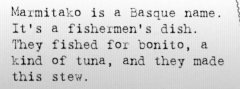

Marmitako is a Basque name. It's a fishermen's dish. They fished for bonito, a kind of tuna, and they made this stew.

# *Purru Salda*

## Basque Leek Soup

| | |
|---|---|
| 2 tablespoons olive oil | About 1 lb. pork ribs, or 12 oz. dried |
| 2 medium leeks | boneless salt cod** |
| 4 medium red potatoes, cut into | 4 cups water |
| bite-sized pieces | 2 teaspoons salt |
| 2 to 3 medium carrots, sliced | 1 bay leaf |
| 1/2 lb. winter squash, peeled, cubed* | |

1. Heat oil in large soup pot over medium heat until hot. Cut leeks into 3-inch slices; quarter lengthwise. Add to soup pot; sauté slowly 5 to 10 minutes or until wilted.
2. Add all remaining ingredients. Bring to a boil. Reduce heat; cover and simmer about 30 minutes or until vegetables are tender.
3. Remove bay leaf and pork ribs. Cut meat off ribs; return to soup pot.

*To make squash easier to peel, heat in microwave for several minutes. Cool slightly; peel.

**To use salt cod, cover with cold water; refrigerate 24 hours, changing water 4 times. Drain well; press with paper towels to remove excess moisture. Remove and discard skin and membranes; cut cod into pieces.

6 to 8 servings

Wonderful! Loved the pork flavor.

Taster

Bacalao. Mercat de la Boqueria, Barcelona

The quality of salt cod (bacalao) and its ready availability in Spain cannot be matched in most parts of the United States. Still, it's worth the hunt; salt cod can often be found in specialty supermarkets, or in Mediterranean markets (Greek, Spanish, Italian). For some of the recipes in this book, when the fish is to be cooked, fresh cod or other white fish can be substituted for salt cod. The spirit and seasoning of the dish remain the same and the results are delicious. For salads and first courses, when the fish is only soaked to remove the salt and not cooked, salt cod is essential. Salt cod keeps very well in the refrigerator.

*Calendaria Hernández Linares (Lala)*

*"In the days when there were no refrigerators, fishermen covered the fish with salt and kept it in baskets inside the house. It lasted a long time."*

*Ferran Adrià*

*"I love salt cod. I love it. In Catalunya and in Basque Country they cook the best bacalao in the world. Yes, yes. In the U.S. they don't have cod of this quality, nor in any place in Europe. The best cod in the world is Norwegian. There's an old culture that wants it. It's a very special tradition because it came from the poor community. Not now. It's not such a cheap product—depending on supply and demand."*

# Txipirones en Su Tinta

## Squid in Black Ink Sauce

*Nekane Berasategui*
*Restaurante Alkatene, Berango, Vizcaya*

"I've loved to cook ever since I was a child. I learned a little from my mother and the rest. But, since I like it, I just try things until I know how. What I cook is traditional Basque food. Basque cooking stands firm ... home cooking with food from our own gardens. We generally don't use spices, just paprika, peppers, parsley, garlic, onion."

*4 tablespoons olive oil*

*1 medium red onion, chopped*

*1 medium carrot, chopped*

*1 garlic clove, chopped*

*1 teaspoon salt*

*1 lb. small squid (about 2 1/2 inches long)*

*Squid ink\**

*2 (3/8-inch-thick) slices baguette*

*1 to 3 tablespoons water*

1. Heat 2 tablespoons of the oil in large skillet over medium heat until hot. Add onion, carrot, garlic and salt; sauté until vegetables are softened.
2. Rinse squid; pat dry. Add squid to skillet; sauté about 2 minutes or until opaque. Remove squid from skillet; place in bowl.
3. Stir remaining 2 tablespoons oil, squid ink and baguette slices into vegetable mixture in skillet until sauce thickens. Place sauce in food processor or blender; process until smooth. Return to skillet; add water or any juice from squid to make a medium sauce consistency.
4. Return squid to skillet. Reduce heat; cover and simmer 30 minutes or until squid are tender.

*Squid ink can be found at specialty food stores or fish markets. The squid ink will turn the sauce a black color. For this recipe, a 0.3-oz. package was used.

4 servings

One of my faves in Spain, and delicious here too.

# Cocido de Alubias Rojas

## Basque Red Bean Stew

| | |
|---|---|
| 1 lb. dried red beans | 1 teaspoon salt |
| 8 cups water | 1 tablespoon olive oil |
| 1 lb. pork ribs | 1 medium onion, chopped |
| 1/4 lb. chorizo | 6 garlic cloves, chopped |
| 1/4 lb. salt pork | 1/4 cup chopped, bottled spicy chiles |
| 8 medium red potatoes peeled, cut into pieces | (such as guindillas or jalapeños) |

1. Soak beans overnight in water to cover. Drain just before using.
2. Bring 8 cups water to a boil in large soup pot or Dutch oven. Add drained beans, pork ribs, chorizo, salt pork, potatoes and salt. Return to a boil. Reduce heat; cover and simmer 3 hours or until beans are softened and potatoes have dissolved to thicken stew, stirring occasionally.
3. Remove pork ribs, chorizo and salt pork from soup pot. Remove meat from bones; slice chorizo and salt pork. Return to soup pot.
4. Toward end of cooking time, heat oil in skillet over medium heat until hot. Add onion, garlic and chiles; cook until softened, stirring occasionally. Stir into stew; cook a few minutes to blend flavors.

8 to 10 servings

Something that's eaten a lot here is beans. This is a cocido that's quite hearty and rich, more for winter than summer. At the end I put in a sofrito of onion, garlic and guindillas (hot peppers).

*Market, A Coruña*

# Lomo Relleno

## Stuffed Pork Tenderloin

2-3 tablespoons olive oil.
*1 medium onion, chopped*
*1 medium carrot, diced*
*1 tomato, peeled, seeded and chopped\**
*1 garlic clove, chopped*
*2 tablespoons chopped fresh parsley*
*1 (3/4 to 1-lb.) pork tenderloin*
*2 oz. thinly-sliced cheese (such as*
  *Manchego, Parmesan, Gruyère*
  *or provolone)*

*2 oz. deli-cut prosciutto or serrano ham*
*1 egg, beaten*
*Flour for dusting*
*1 cup water*
*1 tablespoon water, if desired*
*1 tablespoon flour, if desired*

1. Heat 1 tablespoon of the oil in large skillet over medium heat until hot. Add onion, carrot, tomato, garlic and parsley; sauté until onion and carrot are tender.
2. Meanwhile, cut pork tenderloin in half lengthwise. Place cheese and ham slices down center of one half; top with other half. Tie together with string. Dip tenderloin in beaten egg; dust with flour.
3. Push onion mixture in skillet to sides. Add remaining 1 to 2 tablespoons oil. Add tenderloin; brown on all sides.
4. Stir in 1 cup water. Bring to a boil. Reduce heat; cover and simmer 10 minutes, turning tenderloin at least once. Tenderloin is done when no longer pink in center and internal temperature reaches 160°F.
5. Drizzle sauce over pork tenderloin. If a thicker sauce is desired, in small bowl, blend 1 tablespoon water and 1 tablespoon flour. Add to mixture in skillet; bring to a boil. Reduce heat; simmer, uncovered, until sauce has thickened.

*See page 35.

4 servings

Market, A Coruña

My specialty is main dishes. For desserts, since I don't like them, I don't have many recipes. This dish is very popular here.

Cocinero COOK

# Arroz con Leche

## Rice Pudding

*Angelines and María Dolores Celaya*

"We like to sample things. But, of course, there are limits. We like main dishes, whatever they are ... and sweets. What we need least!"

> 8 cups whole milk
> 2 thin slices lemon peel
> 1 cinnamon stick
> 1/2 cup short-grain (Arborio) rice
> 1/2 cup sugar
> Cinnamon

1. Bring milk, lemon peel and cinnamon stick to a boil in large saucepan. Add rice and sugar; stir well to prevent rice grains from sticking together.
2. Reduce heat; simmer, uncovered, about 2 1/2 to 3 hours, stirring every 10 to 15 minutes. When done, pudding should be consistency of soft custard. If pudding has not thickened sufficiently, boil over high heat for a few minutes, stirring constantly, until it reaches desired consistency. Pudding will thicken slightly as it cools. Cool to room temperature, stirring occasionally.
3. Divide pudding into individual dessert dishes. Sprinkle each with cinnamon. Refrigerate until serving time.

6 servings

The lemon is optional. It gives it a very distinct flavor. Once it's done you can decorate with a little cinnamon. Or put a little cookie on top.

# Espaguetis con Almejas

## Spaghetti with Fresh Clams

*Cristina Alvarez*

"Everything I know how to do I learned from my mother."

| | |
|---|---|
| 2 lb. small clams | 1 jalapeño chile, minced |
| 8 oz. spaghetti | 1 tablespoon flour |
| 1/4 cup olive oil | 1 cup dry white wine |
| 1 large red bell pepper, chopped | Salt and freshly ground pepper |
| 4 garlic cloves, chopped | |

1. Scrub clams under cold running water. Set aside.
2. Heat oil in large skillet over medium heat until hot. Add bell pepper, garlic and chile; sauté until softened, stirring constantly.
3. Reduce heat; stir in flour until smooth. Stir in wine and clams. Bring to a boil. Reduce heat; cover and cook 5 to 10 minutes or until clams open. As clams open, remove from skillet and set aside.
4. Cook spaghetti according to package directions, or until it is al dente. Drain immediately.
5. Meanwhile, when spaghetti is almost done, return clams to skillet. Season to taste with salt and pepper. Warm clam mixture and stir into drained spaghetti.

4 first-course servings

Freshly ground pepper is a nice addition to this dish.

# *Rape a la Americana*

## Monkfish with Savory Tomato Sauce

*José Madrid*

"These recipes are made a lot around here in Basque Country. A lot."

| | |
|---|---|
| *3 tablespoons olive oil* | *1/4 teaspoon pepper* |
| *1 medium onion, chopped* | *6 to 8 large shrimp with shells* |
| *1 (28-oz.) can crushed tomatoes, undrained* | *1 1/2 lb. monkfish (about 8 pieces)\** |
| *1/2 teaspoon sugar* | *Flour* |
| *1/2 teaspoon salt* | |

1. Heat 1 tablespoon of the oil in large skillet over medium heat until hot. Add onion; sauté until it begins to turn golden. Reduce heat; stir in tomatoes; simmer 5 minutes.
2. Cool tomato mixture slightly; put through strainer or food mill. Return mixture to skillet; stir in sugar, salt and pepper.
3. Rinse shrimp; remove shells. Add shells to tomato sauce in skillet; reserve shrimp. Bring tomato sauce to a boil. Reduce heat; simmer 20 minutes.
4. Cool mixture slightly; put mixture through strainer or food mill to remove shells. Set tomato sauce aside.
5. Heat remaining 2 tablespoons oil in large skillet over medium heat. Add shrimp; sauté 2 to 3 minutes or until opaque, stirring constantly. Remove shrimp from skillet.
6. Rinse monkfish; pat dry. Dust monkfish with flour to coat. Add to skillet; cook 3 to 4 minutes on each side or until fish flakes easily with fork. Add shrimp and tomato sauce; simmer 2 to 3 minutes to combine flavors.

\*Monkfish has a consistency similar to shellfish.

4 servings

A fabulous sauce; worth the extra effort.

Taster

# *Merluza a la Sidra*

## Hake in Cider Sauce

*2 tablespoons olive oil*
*1 medium onion, finely chopped*
*2 garlic cloves, chopped*
*1 teaspoon flour*
*2 cups hard apple cider (with alcohol)*
*1 1/2 to 2-lb. fish fillets (such as hake, cod, haddock or halibut)*

1. Heat oil in large skillet over medium heat until hot. Add onion and garlic; sauté until softened.
2. Stir in flour until well blended. Stir in cider. Bring to a boil. Reduce heat; simmer 20 minutes.
3. Meanwhile, rinse fish; pat dry.
4. Add fish to skillet. Simmer 4 to 5 minutes or until fish flakes easily with fork. (If fillets are thin, handle carefully.)

4 servings

Though hake is a Spanish favorite, beloved for its delicate flavor and flaky texture, it is not widely available in the U.S. Cod or haddock is an excellent substitute.

Autora
Author

# Castilla y León

The provinces of Castilla y León are: Avila, Burgos, León, Palencia, Salamanca, Segovia, Soria, Valladolid and Zamora.

The cultural importance of food has been understood for centuries in Castilla y León, and has played a part in making the region a popular destination. Though each of the nine provinces has its particular specialties, many recipes cross provincial borders, for example, **Cocido**. This hearty dish is served in three parts—first a rich broth simmered with noodles; second, garbanzos and potatoes; and finally, a variety of meats, sausage, chicken, and meatballs or dumplings. **Sopa Castellana**, a savory soup made with bread, ham, poached eggs and garlic is another such recipe. As is Bacalao al Ajo Arriero, or "Mule Driver" Cod, so called because it was the mule drivers who carried the recipe from one place to another.

Avila province is home to perhaps the oldest breed of cattle in Europe. It is also a producer of goat's-milk cheese, figs, cherries, peppers and a famous egg yolk treat, Yemas de Santa Teresa, which has been made for centuries by nuns. (The whites of the eggs were originally used to clarify Cebreros wines.)

Burgos is known for baby lamb, legumes, wild mushrooms, snails and Queso de Burgos, a fresh sheep's-milk cheese which is delicious with quince paste. Burgos's morcilla has been a specialty since the 18th century when Valencian rice was mixed into the recipe.

*Suckling pig from a wood-burning oven*

León's culinary history goes back to the lords and rich monasteries of the Middle Ages; few provinces offer such plenty and diversity. Fifty commercial enterprises alone are involved in making Cecina de León, a centuries-old recipe for cured, dried and smoked beef. Botillo, once a meal for the poor, is now a very popular dish: meat from the tail, ribs and jaw of the pig is put into the pig's stomach and cooked with potatoes and vegetables.

Among Palencia's noteworthy recipes are garlic soup, pigeon stewed with greens, and **Menestra de Verduras**, a vegetable stew enjoyed throughout Spain.

Salamanca has three universities, including the oldest in Spain, founded in 1218. Sixty percent of the nation's Ibérico ham is produced in Salamanca, where dry cold winters are perfect for salting and drying the meat naturally. Local culinary standouts include Chanfaina Salmantina made with rice, giblets, lamb sweetbreads and chorizo; Farinato—sausage fried and served with eggs; and the crunchy sugar-coated almonds, **Almendras Garrapiñadas**.

Once a hub of textiles and cattle, Segovia is now a culinary center, known for its wood-burning roasting ovens and the high quality and perfect preparation of its Lechazo, baby lamb, and Cochinillo, suckling pig (which is roasted until the exact moment it can be separated into servings with the edge of a plate). Other specialties include Gamo con Setas, venison with mushrooms; and Jabalí con Arándonos, wild boar with black currant sauce.

From Soria comes Migas del Pastor, made with bread bits, green pepper, oil and garlic. Soria's chorizo is non-traditional (a blend of beef and pork), as is the morcilla made with raisins and cinnamon that's baked and eaten for dessert.

Valladolid is famous for sausages, pine nuts, garbanzos, sea bream (introduced in the 14th century when a way was opened to the Cantabrian Sea), chicory, endive, Tudela asparagus, and the sheep's-milk cheese known as Pata de Mulo.

The river Duero divides Zamora into the Land of Bread and the Land of Wine. Zamora is well-known for Queso Zamorano, a sheep's-milk cheese, salmon-colored trout, and lean Aliste beef. Dishes to try include Ancas de Rana, frogs' legs, and Pulpo a la Sanabresa, octopus served with a zesty mojo sauce.

Outstanding wines include: Ribera del Duero reds, Rueda whites and sparkling wines, Cigales clarets and fruity rosés, Bierzo with varieties that date from Roman times, and Vinos de Toro—deep-colored reds drunk either young or aged in oak. It is said that Valdevimbre Los Oteros, an artesenal rosé, was the wine favored by the Russian Czars.

*Carbonero el Mayor. Castilla y León*

*Mesón El Drago. Tegueste. Tenerife*

In Spain, cheese making has evolved over the centuries and has had many cultural influences: the Romans who understood the process of coagulation and the use of salt as a preservative, the Arabs who improved Spanish livestock, and the Germanic and Celtic peoples who settled in the fertile Atlantic regions. Today, there are over 100 varieties of Spanish cheese to sample and enjoy.

Spain's climate and topography make it an ideal place for different types of goats and an extraordinary number of goat's-milk cheeses, including Ibores (Extremadura), Garrotxa (Catalunya), Majorero (Islas Canarias), and Rondeño (Andalucía).

Even more representative of Spanish livestock are sheep. With their migration patterns they can reach the best pastures and grazing lands. Best known among sheep's-milk cheeses are Manchego (Castilla la Mancha), Idiazabal (País Vasco and Navarra), Roncal (Navarra), Zamorano (Castilla y León), and La Serena (Extremadura).

Cows are more common to the humid Atlantic areas, but are also found in mountainous regions. In cow's-milk cheeses, look for: Mahon (Islas Baleares); Nata Cantabria, Quesuco, and Ahumado de Aliva (Cantabria); Tetilla, Ulloa, San Simón, and Cebreiro (Galicia); and Cabrales (Asturias).

The milk from goats, sheep and cows is often mixed as well, for example, in the cheeses called Tronchon (Aragón and Valencia), Iberico (Castilla la Mancha), and Picón (Castilla y León).

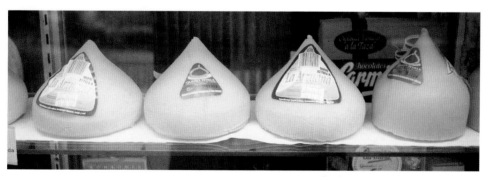

*Tetilla cheese. Santiago de Compostela*

53

# Cocido

## Classic One-Pot Meal

*Lucía (Sofía) Herrero Lázaro*

"I got my recipes from my grandmother and my mother, and now I'm continuing the tradition with my daughter-in-law. Some things I cook differently from her mother and if she's eating at my house and it's something she likes, she says, 'Lucía, how did you make such and such? I like it.' Naturally, I tell her. But cooking never comes out exactly the same. It's like when I go to the beauty shop, the hairdo is never quite the same."

### Soup

3 cups dried garbanzo beans
1 ham bone or smoked ham shank
1 (1 1/2-lb.) beef or veal shank
1 lb. pork shoulder
2 oz. salt pork
1 medium onion, chopped
2 teaspoons salt
1 bay leaf
12 cups water
1 lb. chicken thighs, skin removed
5 medium baking potatoes,
  peeled, cut into pieces
1/2 lb. chorizo
1 cup thin egg noodles

### Dumplings

1 egg, beaten
1/2 cup bread crumbs
1 garlic clove, finely chopped
1 tablespoon finely chopped
  fresh parsley
1/8 teaspoon salt
2 tablespoons olive oil

1. Soak beans overnight in water to cover. Drain just before using.
2. In large soup pot or Dutch oven, combine ham bone, beef shank, pork shoulder, salt pork, onion, salt, bay leaf and 12 cups water. Bring to a boil; skim off foam. Cover; simmer 1 hour.*
3. Add drained beans and chicken. Return to a boil. Reduce heat; cover and simmer 1 hour.
4. Meanwhile, prepare dumplings. In large bowl, combine all dumpling ingredients except oil; mix well. Shape into 8 balls. Heat oil in large skillet over medium-high heat until hot. Add dumplings; cook until light golden brown, turning frequently.
5. Remove 6 cups broth from soup pot; pour through strainer. Reserve broth. (This will be boiled separately with noodles for first course.)
6. Add potatoes, chorizo and dumplings to soup pot; cook 15 to 20 minutes or until potatoes are tender. Remove bay leaf before serving.
7. To serve: for first course, boil egg noodles in reserved broth; for second course, place garbanzo beans and potatoes in serving bowl; for third course, place meats on platter.

*At this point, soup can be removed from heat, cooled and refrigerated overnight. Skim off fat before returning to heat.

8 to 10 servings

It depends on the ingredients you use. The chickens that we produce are running around the yard. The ham I have is from my pigs. We cure it ourselves at home.

Cocinero COOK

# Sopa Castellana

## Castilian Garlic Soup

| | |
|---|---|
| 2 tablespoons olive oil | 1 teaspoon salt |
| 4 garlic cloves, chopped | 1/2 teaspoon paprika |
| 2 chorizos, sliced | 4 eggs |
| 4 cups water | 4 (1/2-inch-thick) slices toasted day-old |
| 3 to 4 oz. prosciutto or serrano ham, cubed |    bread, cubed |

1. Heat oil in large saucepan over medium heat until hot. Add garlic; sauté slowly until golden.
2. Add chorizo; brown. Add water, ham, salt and paprika. Bring to a boil. Reduce heat; cover and simmer 5 minutes.
3. Break eggs, one by one, into saucer. Slide eggs gently into soup; arrange bread cubes around eggs. Cover; simmer an additional 5 minutes or until eggs are poached There is no bay leaf in the recipe, Divide eggs, bread cubes and soup into individual soup bowls.

4 servings

It just keeps getting better! Beautifully simple soup with a kick.

Taster

# Flan de Leche Condensada

## Quick Flan

> 6 tablespoons sugar
> 1 teaspoon water
> 6 eggs
> 2 1/2 cups whole milk
> 1 (14-oz.) can sweetened condensed milk

1. Heat oven to 325°F. Caramelize sugar by placing the sugar and water in heavy, medium skillet or saucepan. (Adding water will help sugar melt more evenly.) Heat over medium heat, stirring constantly with heat-resistant spoon, until sugar is melted and becomes golden.
2. Immediately pour caramelized sugar into 6-cup shallow mold. Spread over bottom of mold. (Work quickly and carefully, using potholders, as caramel will make mold become extremely hot. It is okay if caramelized sugar does not cover entire bottom of mold; it will melt as flan bakes.)
3. Lightly beat eggs in medium bowl. Stir in milk and sweetened condensed milk. Pour over caramelized sugar in mold. Place mold in shallow pan of hot water.
4. Bake 40 to 50 minutes or until knife inserted in center comes out clean. Cool. Cover; refrigerate until serving time. (Flan can be made a day ahead.)
5. To serve, run knife around edge of mold; invert flan onto shallow serving plate.

8 servings

Excellent, excellent, so creamy and rich (but not too rich).

Taster

*Market, A Coruña*

### José María Ramos

"Though their ingredients are similar, the cocidos in Spain are very different. In Castilla, Salamanca, Madrid, and in the whole region of Castilla y León, cocido is basically garbanzos cooked with pork, cured pork products, chicken, or more typically, hen, and veal meat from the ribs—meat with a little fat. The codillo, the top joint of the foreleg, is also used. In Galicia they use beans, and as an accompaniment, greens and 'cachelos,' which are whole peeled potatoes.

In Castilla they eat the garbanzos first with the potatoes, and next what's called the 'tajadas,' the chunks and slices of the meats from the cocido. In Galicia everything is eaten together: the greens, the potatoes, the beans and the meat, all in the same plate. You serve yourself what you want.

In Galicia it's customary to eat the soup from the cocido afterward. A cup of cocido as they say, eh? But there's no rule that says, 'first the soup and then the cocido.' In some restaurants, they serve the cocido first and then the soup. In other places, it's the reverse.

Cocido is a filling dish, very filling. It's always accompanied with red wine, but a wine with less alcoholic strength; when you eat a lot, you have to drink a lot. Here, in Galicia, the cocido goes better with local wines, young wines from the growers. If you're going to eat cocido, you need a lot to drink."

# Madrid

Capital of Spain since 1562, Madrid is also the geographic center of the Peninsula. Its altitude, 650 meters (2,133 feet), and proximity to the surrounding mountains make for hot summers and chilly winters. Monumental Madrid, the heart of the city, was mainly built during the Hapsburg reign (16th and 17th centuries). It is also home to the Prado, an 18th century structure, which is one of the world's most important and most spectacular museums.

La Platería, Madrid

When Madrid became the country's capital, there was extensive immigration, and with the people came their traditions. You might say Madrid's cuisine is the best of local recipes, enhanced by all the regional dishes of Spain. It is also an interesting fusion of foods from the royalty with those of the middle and working classes. Today, new ideas continue to arrive from all over the world.

Perhaps Madrid's best-known dish is its unique version of Cocido—a combination of meats, marrow bones, garbanzos, potatoes, cabbage, turnips, bacon, chorizo and meatballs. It was once eaten practically every day until some ingredients became too expensive and preparation time deemed too long. Another Madrileño specialty is Sopa de Ajo, the garlic soup that is a winter staple in many bars. Though it, too, is prepared throughout Spain, in Madrid it holds a place of honor.

Other notable dishes include Callos a la Madrileña, beef tripe, blood sausage and ham simmered in a savory tomato sauce; Tortilla Española (**Tortilla de Patata**), an omelet cooked Madrid-style with potatoes and onions; and **Estofado**, garlicky, slow-cooked meat cooked with vegetables and spices. Judías Tío Lucas,

a hearty, long-simmered bean dish, has been popular in Madrid for over a century. It was created by a Sevillian barman, Tío Lucas, whose pub was frequented by actors, bullfighters and aristocrats.

Despite its inland location, Madrid has much to offer fish lovers, including the second largest fish market in the world. Probably the first ocean fish known in Madrid was bacalao, salt cod. In the local recipe, Soldaditos de Pavía, the bacalao is batter-fried with red pepper strips that are said to resemble the plumes worn in the caps of the Hussars of Pavía. Another of Madrid's delicious gifts to fish aficionados is **Besugo al Horno**, oven-roasted porgy, a traditional Christmas dish now enjoyed all year long.

Breakfast for many Madrileños is churros (fritters) dipped in coffee or thick chocolate. A mid-morning snack might include a glass of beer or wine served with black olives spiced with vinegar, onions, and paprika. Late afternoon is time for tapas. And, for those who like the late scene, Madrid's pubs, cafe-theaters, and discos are open till dawn.

Madrid was once a city surrounded by wine—not only in the shops, but in the fields which have become an industrial zone. Where the airport now stands were the vineyards of Valdepeñas, a wine currently enjoying a revival. Madrid's Denominaciones de Origen, almost all young wines, are Navalcarnero, a sweet garnacha wine with a high alcohol content; Arganda, a delicious white that goes well with fish; and the stronger wines of San Martín de Valdeiglesias which can easily reach a 14% alcohol content.

*Sunday afternoon in Madrid (opposite)*

# Patatas a la Riojana

## Spicy Rioja Potatoes

*Isabel Seivane*

"I learned to cook by experience. My children were boarding students with the nuns in Cadiz. I went with them to help in the kitchen and I was there for seven years. I cooked a lot of fish! ... I used to watch a cook on television, and a lot of things stayed in my head. I cut out things from the newspaper, too."

| | |
|---|---|
| 1 1/2 lb. small potatoes | 1 teaspoon salt |
| 1/3 cup olive oil | 1/2 lb. chorizo, sliced |
| 1 large onion, sliced | 1/2 cup dry white wine |
| 2 garlic cloves, finely chopped | Water |
| 2 medium red bell peppers, chopped | 2 bottled spicy whole chiles (such as |
| 1 tablespoon paprika | guindillas or jalapeños) |

1. Cut potatoes halfway through, then "snap" open.
2. Heat oil in large skillet over medium heat until hot. Add potatoes; cook about 10 minutes or until golden brown, stirring occasionally.
3. Add onion and garlic; cook about 5 minutes or until onion is slightly brown, stirring frequently.
4. Stir in bell peppers, paprika and salt; cook 2 minutes, stirring occasionally.
5. Stir in chorizo and wine; cook about 3 minutes or until wine is slightly reduced.
6. Add water to cover vegetables; add spicy chiles. Bring to a boil. Reduce heat; simmer about 15 minutes or until potatoes are tender. Remove chiles. Spoon into individual flat soup bowls.

6 servings

You have to 'chascar' (crack) the potatoes; cut them halfway through and snap them open. This allows the potatoes to absorb the flavor better.

# Sopa de Calabaza con Almejas

## Squash Soup with Clams

| | |
|---|---|
| *18 medium clams* | *1 medium onion, chopped* |
| *6 medium prawns or large shrimp* | *1 medium green bell pepper, diced* |
| *in shells* | *1 medium tomato, halved, grated* |
| *4 tablespoons olive oil* | *1 medium leek, sliced* |
| *1 lb. winter squash, peeled, cubed\** | *4 cups water* |
| *2 medium carrots, diced* | *2 teaspoons salt* |
| *2 medium red potatoes, diced* | *2 garlic cloves, sliced* |

1. Scrub clams under cold running water. Rinse prawns; drain.
2. Heat 2 tablespoons of the oil in large saucepan or Dutch oven over medium heat until hot. Add squash, carrots, potatoes, onion, bell pepper, tomato and leek; cook until softened.
3. Add water and salt. Bring to a boil. Reduce heat; cover and simmer 20 minutes or until all vegetables are tender. Cool slightly.
4. Purée vegetable mixture in food processor or blender. (This may need to be done in several batches.) Return to saucepan and keep warm.
5. Heat remaining 2 tablespoons oil in large skillet over medium-high heat until hot. Add garlic, clams and prawns; cover and cook until clams open and prawns are opaque, stirring frequently. Drain clams and prawns.
6. Spoon soup into individual soup bowls; divide clams and prawns; add to soup.

*To make squash easier to peel, heat in microwave for several minutes. Cool slightly, peel.

6 servings

It's expensive because of the clams, but very nourishing. ... I like to cook and experiment.

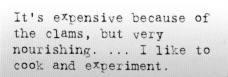

# Besugo al Horno

## Oven-Baked Porgy, Madrid Style

3 to 4 lb. whole fish (such as porgy, snapper or sea bass), cleaned, scaled and scored
2 tablespoons olive oil
6 medium baking potatoes, peeled, cut into 1/4-inch-thick slices
Salt and freshly ground pepper

2 medium onions, cut into 1/8 to 1/4-inch-thick slices
3 garlic cloves, thinly sliced
6 sprigs fresh parsley
1 tablespoon bread crumbs
1/2 cup dry sherry
1 to 2 teaspoons olive oil

1. Heat oven to 375°F. Lightly oil large baking dish. Rinse fish; pat dry. Sprinkle with salt. Set aside.
2. Heat oil in large skillet over medium heat until hot. Add potatoes; sauté about 15 minutes or until softened. Season to taste with salt and pepper. Arrange potatoes in baking dish.
3. If necessary, add more oil to same skillet. Add onions; sauté until softened. Arrange over potatoes in baking dish.
4. In food processor or with mortar and pestle, process garlic and parsley. Stuff most of mixture into scored part of fish, reserving a little.
5. Top potatoes and onions with fish; sprinkle with bread crumbs. Pour sherry into pan and sprinkle 1 to 2 teaspoons oil over fish. Top with reserved garlic and parsley mixture.
6. Bake 20 to 25 minutes or until fish flakes easily with fork. Test for doneness by inserting an instant-read thermometer into thickest part of fish. Fish is done when temperature is 140°F. If it has not reached 140°F., return fish to oven and watch carefully since temperature will rise quickly.

6 servings

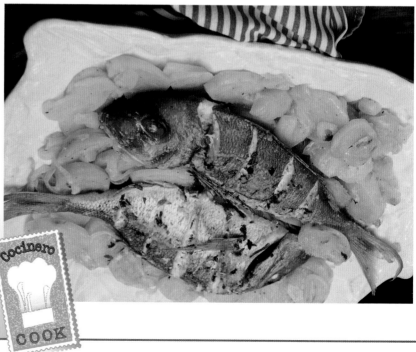

Of course, things aren't like they were before, life isn't either. Women work, they don't have time to cook; everything is more hurried. ... This is a very healthy, simple meal and everybody likes it.

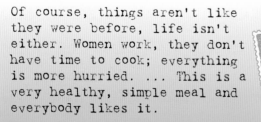

# *Lombarda*

## Festive Red Cabbage

*3 tablespoons olive oil*

*2 lb. red cabbage, coarsely chopped (about 6 cups)*

*2 garlic cloves, finely chopped*

*1 1/2 teaspoons salt*

*1/3 cup red wine vinegar*

*Freshly ground pepper*

1. Heat oil in large skillet over medium heat until hot. Add cabbage, garlic and salt; cook 10 minutes, stirring frequently.
2. Reduce heat; cover and cook about 10 minutes or until cabbage is tender.
3. Stir in vinegar; sprinkle with pepper.

6 servings

Whatever the earth grows is cooked. ...This is a traditional Christmas Eve dish, when red cabbage is available.

# Berenjena a la Parrilla

## Broiled Stuffed Eggplant

*Ellanor Ravenga*

"The eggplant recipes are easy, cheap and good."

**2 medium eggplants**
**2 tablespoons olive oil**
**1 1/2 teaspoons salt**
**1 medium tomato, peeled, seeded and chopped***
**1 teaspoon dried oregano**
**1/4 teaspoon red pepper flakes, if desired**
**Freshly grated Parmesan cheese to taste**

1. Heat oven to 375°F. Grease cookie sheet. Cut eggplants in half lengthwise; place on greased cookie sheet. Sprinkle with 1 tablespoon of the oil and 1 teaspoon of the salt. Bake 20 minutes or until tender. Cool.
2. Scoop flesh from center of eggplants; reserve shells. Cut flesh into bite-sized pieces.
3. Heat remaining tablespoon oil in large skillet over medium heat until hot. Add eggplant, tomato, oregano, red pepper flakes and remaining 1/2 teaspoon salt; sauté slowly until eggplant is tender.
4. Fill eggplant shells with mixture; sprinkle with cheese. Broil 3 to 5 minutes or until cheese is golden brown.

*See page 35.

4 servings

The perfect amount of chile peppers.

# *Berenjena San Jacobo*

## Eggplant Saint James

| | |
|---|---|
| *1 large or 2 medium eggplants* | *Flour* |
| *Salt* | *2 eggs, beaten* |
| *Olive oil* | *Bread crumbs* |
| *Fresh mozzarella or queso blanco* | *Freshly ground pepper* |
| *cheese slices* | *Oil for frying* |

1. Cut eggplants crosswise into 1/2-inch-thick slices; arrange in layers in colander, salting each layer well. Let stand at room temperature for 30 minutes.
2. Drain eggplant slices; dry with paper towels. Place slices in single layer on cookie sheet. Brush with oil. Broil about 3 minutes on each side. Cool slightly.
3. Make sandwiches by placing 1 slice of cheese between 2 eggplant slices. Dust each sandwich with flour; dip in beaten egg. Coat with bread crumbs. Season to taste with salt and pepper.
4. Heat 3/4 inch of oil in large skillet over high heat until very hot. Fry sandwiches in hot oil until golden brown on both sides. Remove from skillet; drain on paper towels. Cut into pieces for tapas or serve whole as a side dish.

4 side-dish servings or 8 tapas

In Spanish, for reasons unknown, anything filled with ham or cheese or both is called San Jacobo or Saint James. ... This can be cut into smaller pieces to make a great tapa.

# Mayonesa

## Mayonnaise

2 egg yolks

2 tablespoons lemon juice (1/2 to 1 lemon)

1/4 teaspoon salt

1/4 teaspoon white wine vinegar

1 cup extra virgin olive oil

For best results, use chilled ingredients.

By Machine:

1. Place egg yolks in blender or mixer bowl; blend a few seconds. Add lemon juice, salt and vinegar; blend well.
2. With motor running, very slowly add oil, blending until thickened and silky.

By Hand:

1. Place egg yolks in mortar or bowl; whip with wire whisk. Add lemon juice, salt and vinegar; blend well.
2. Very slowly add oil, mixing until thickened and silky.

Keeps for 3 or 4 days in the refrigerator.

Makes 1 1/4 cups

Bottle this and I'd have it in my fridge!

Taster

# Gazpacho Andaluz

## Classic Gazpacho from Andalucía

*Caridad San Román*

"These are very old recipes, recipes of a lifetime. People didn't travel as much before."

### Gazpacho

3 (1-inch-thick) slices French bread

4-5 medium tomatoes, peeled, seeded and cut in pieces*

1 medium cucumber, peeled, seeded and cut in pieces

1 medium red or green bell pepper, cut in pieces

2 garlic cloves, chopped

1/3 cup olive oil

2 tablespoons white wine vinegar

1 teaspoon salt

1/2 teaspoon cumin

### Garnishes

Diced cucumber

Diced green bell pepper

Diced tomato

Chopped onion

Chopped hard-cooked egg

1. Soak bread in 1 cup water for about 30 minutes.
2. Meanwhile, in food processor or blender, process tomatoes, cucumber, bell pepper and garlic until no large pieces remain.
3. Squeeze bread dry; crumble. Mix bread with oil, vinegar, salt and cumin. Add to vegetable mixture; blend. If gazpacho is too thick, add a little water. Taste for seasoning; if desired, add more salt and cumin.
4. Force gazpacho through strainer or food mill. Refrigerate 2 to 4 hours or until very well chilled before serving.
5. Serve in glasses as a beverage or in bowls as a soup with desired garnishes.

*See page 35.

4 servings

Great summer soup—loved being able to drink it from a glass.

Taster

# Sopa de Arroz y Mariscos

## Rice and Seafood Soup

| | |
|---|---|
| *1 lb. small clams* | *1 teaspoon salt* |
| *1/2 lb. shrimp, shelled, deveined* | *1 teaspoon paprika* |
| *2 tablespoons olive oil* | *3 cups water* |
| *2 garlic cloves, chopped* | *1/4 cup short-grain (Arborio) rice* |
| *1 medium tomato, peeled, diced** | *1/4 cup chopped fresh parsley* |

1. Scrub clams under cold running water. Rinse shrimp; drain.
2. Heat oil in large saucepan over medium heat until hot. Add garlic; sauté until slightly golden. Add tomato; sauté an additional few minutes. Stir in salt and paprika.
3. Add water and rice. Bring to a boil. Reduce heat; simmer 10 minutes.
4. Add clams, shrimp and parsley. Return to a boil. Reduce heat; simmer 10 minutes or until shrimp is opaque, rice is tender and clams open.

*See page 35.

4 servings

Flavors are perfect.
Loved this.

Taster

Embotits Bundo, L 'Arboç, Tarragona

Herman Lamarca
Caralps

"In Spain, ham is eaten at all hours and in all places. Originally, centuries ago, ham was developed out of necessity. It was the easiest way to preserve big pieces of meat for eating later. As the years passed, need became gastronomy, and as people traveled between towns, they were able to compare the various methods of curing that coexisted in the Peninsula. This is what is known today as the ham culture.

In fact, curing ham is a combination of two conservation techniques to get rid of the moisture: drying and salting. When the pig is killed, it's hung on an incline for one day, then put in a container filled to the brim with salt, and tilted with a weight on top so it releases its juice. After that, it's hung in a cool, dry place—the high mountains, for example. Of course, since there aren't many such places, and because consumption is up, the traditional manner of drying can't be maintained. Today artificial drying with refrigeration is also used.

There are three basic categories of ham. The ham consumed most often is from farm-raised pigs a year and a half old. Part is eaten as fresh meat, while the hindquarters and forequarters are made into ham and paletilla (shoulder blade). It is the most economical ham in Spain, approximately $28-$84 for a whole ham.

After that is the recebo class, pigs raised in captivity that eat part feed and part natural products such as acorns and various types of roots. Recebo is in major production. Unfortunately, what is often called and sold as Iberico, the highest quality ham, is really recebo.

True Iberico is produced in very few parts of Spain, basically in Extremadura. They need huge areas with few animals; it's the animals that are different. The Iberico pig is native to the peninsula; it feeds on 'bellotas,' acorns. To buy an Iberico ham, you have to reserve it almost a year ahead. It can cost $840-$1,120. But it has to be tried. This has to be tried."

69

From the Pyrenees in the north to the Mediterranean coast on the east, Catalunya is a beautiful and culturally-varied land. Its four provinces are Barcelona, Girona, Lleida, and Tarragona.

Since ancient times, Catalunya has been at the crossroads of history, and a port of entry for ideas and influences from France, Italy and beyond, including the latest culinary fashions. It has the country's most sophisticated cooking, and the best documented, historically. A 4th century poet described the popularity of a strong spicy conserve, garum, made with fish entrails, which inspired heavy wine consumption. Arab influence left a taste for almond and fruit pastries and the use of various spices. But actual Catalan cuisine, a blend of the local and the exotic, was formalized only in the 19th century. It is this cuisine which has been preserved and elaborated on by contemporary chefs.

Although each province has its specialties, some key dishes are found throughout Catalunya: **Escalivada**, roasted eggplant and peppers, often accompanied by onions and anchovies; **Pà amb Tomàquet**, toasted bread rubbed with tomato, olive oil, and salt; **Esqueixada**, a refreshing salt cod salad; and the simple yet delicious garden-fresh salad, **Ensalada Catalana**. Many favorite dishes are of humble origin, such as **Habas a la Catalana**, herb-scented fava beans

*Las Ramblas, Barcelona*

with blood sausage; Pato con Nabos, duck with turnips; and Escudella i Carn d'Olla, a stew of meats, beans, vegetables, potatoes and sausage which was eaten almost daily until the 1930s.

Olive oil is essential to Catalan cooking, as is this quartet of sauces: **Samfaina**, a sauté of tomatoes, peppers, eggplant, garlic, and onions; Picada, a mixture of garlic, parsley, toasted almonds, hazelnuts or pine nuts, and oil; **Allioli**, a creamy oil and garlic blend which dates from Roman times; and **Sofrito**, a sautéed garlic, onion and tomato combination used throughout Spain.

On the dessert menu, traditional favorites include **Crema Catalana**, creamy custard with a caramelized sugar top; Mel i Mató, soft, fresh cheese served with honey and walnuts; and **Menja Blanc**, almond cream flavored with lemon and cinnamon.

The long history of Barcelona is evident in its many Romanesque, Gothic and Renaissance monuments, but Modernisme, the characteristic Art Nouveau style which makes it unique, dates only from the past 100 years. The most cosmopolitan of Spanish cities, Barcelona has always been at the forefront of international trends and its restaurants are among the finest in Europe. Whether it's Catalan classics or dishes with a contemporary accent, in Barcelona you can delight in them all.

*Pan de Higos — Fig Cake: Mercat de la Boqueria, Barcelona (opposite)*

Lleida has high peaks, fertile plains, and a trove of Romanesque art to offer visitors. It also presents a deliciously-varied cuisine: trout from mountain rivers, lamb, hare, pork sausages (xolís), a variety of cheeses and game, and the famous olive oils from Garrigues. Lleida is an important center of agriculture, industry and commerce.

Tarragona, capital of the Costa Daurada, was the first Roman city in Spain and capital of Hispania Citerior. Roman walls remain, as do an amphitheater from the first century BC, arches of the Roman circus, and an early Christian necropolis. Tarragona's gastronomy is distinguished as well. **Romesco**, an unforgettable sauce made with almonds, hazelnuts, dried peppers, tomatoes and garlic was created there. Look, also, for **Xató**, an escarole salad with salt cod and tuna; Rossejat de Fideos, fish with thin noodles served with Allioli; omelets with tiny fish called Chanquetes; and

Coca de Recapte, a tender, thin pastry with various toppings.

In the province of Girona, travelers will be charmed by the rugged Costa Brava coastline and the amazing beauty of its cliffs, beaches, and picturesque towns. Food lovers will be seduced as well by a fascinating mix of flavors such as **Sea and Mountain**—chicken simmered with seafood, or Sweet and Salty—duck stuffed with a marvelous mixture of pears, turnips, apples and olives.

Catalunya is among the Peninsula's biggest wine producers and its wines have been renowned since Roman times. There are eight Denominaciones de Origen: Priorat, Conca de Barberà, Alella, Tarragona, Empordà, Costers del Segre, Penedès, and Terra Alta, and one more product which has given modern Catalan viticulture a big boost—sparkling cava, 90% of which is from Penedès.

*Street sign. Sitges*

# *Pà amb Tomàquet*

## Catalan Bread with Tomato

*Nuria Jiménez Uroz*

"In the rest of Spain when you ask for bread with tomato they call you a Catalan. It's like the flag. Or, like spaghetti for the Italians. A little bit the same. This is traditional for almost everybody here."

---

**4 (1/2-inch-thick) slices crusty Italian or French bread**

**4 small to medium tomatoes, halved**

**Salt***

**Extra virgin olive oil**

**Thinly sliced prosciutto or serrano ham, or dry-cured salami**

---

1. Toast bread under broiler or on grill.**
2. Rub and squeeze tomato over toasted bread. Sprinkle with salt; drizzle with oil to taste. Serve with ham or salami.

*Coarse sea salt or kosher salt has the best flavor.

**Toasted bread can be rubbed with halved garlic cloves.

4 servings

A taste of summer in the middle of winter.

Taste

# Pulpo a la Gallega

## Octopus, Galician Style

3/4 to 1 lb. frozen octopus (1 large or 2 small)*
Extra virgin olive oil
Coarse salt
Paprika

1. Wash octopus under cold running water.
2. Bring large pot of water to a boil. Submerge octopus in water; immediately remove. Repeat 2 more times, bringing water to a boil and submerging octopus each time.
3. Return water to a boil. Add octopus to pot; reduce heat and simmer 45 minutes to 1 hour depending on size, or until tender. Drain; cool.
4. Rinse octopus under cold running water to remove any loose skin. Cut body and tentacles into bite-sized pieces; place on serving platter. Drizzle with oil. Sprinkle with salt and paprika. If desired, serve with sliced boiled potatoes.

*Freezing tenderizes the octopus.

4 servings

Cook octopus on a low flame; a high flame removes the skin. Salt should be added after cooking.

# Espinacas a la Catalana

## Spinach with Raisins and Pine Nuts

*1/4 cup raisins*
*1/4 cup pine nuts*
*2 tablespoons olive oil*
*2 lb. fresh spinach, or 3 (10-oz.) pkg. trimmed washed spinach, cooked, drained*
*Salt and freshly ground pepper*

1. Cover raisins with boiling water; let stand 15 minutes to plump. Drain; set raisins aside.
2. Heat large skillet over medium-low heat until hot. Add pine nuts; cook and stir until lightly browned. Remove pine nuts from skillet; set aside.
3. In same skillet, heat oil over medium heat until hot. Add spinach, raisins and pine nuts; cook and stir until thoroughly heated. Season to taste with salt and pepper.

4 servings

Great! The color, texture, complexity, flavor.

Taster

# Empedrat

## Tuna and White Bean Salad

*1 (15.5-oz.) can great northern beans, drained*

*1 (6-oz.) can tuna in olive oil, drained*

*1 to 2 medium tomatoes, chopped*

*1/2 medium onion, chopped*

*1/2 cup pitted black olives (such as kalamata), halved*

**Salt**

1. In medium bowl, combine all ingredients; mix lightly with fork.
2. Cover; refrigerate at least 1 hour.

4 servings

The olives make this dish!

# Patatas Rellenas de Bacalao

## Cod-Stuffed Potatoes

*Sandra Villar*

"I learned to cook from my grandmother. As she always said, 'everything that's made with good things turns out good.' It's harder but I buy everything in specialty shops. I don't like to go to the supermarket."

---

*1/2 lb. dried boneless salt cod*

*16 small potatoes (1 1/2 to 2 inches in diameter)*

*2 anchovies, finely chopped*

*1/2 cup Allioli (Aïoli), page 157*

---

1. Cover salt cod with cold water; refrigerate 24 hours, changing water 4 times.
2. Heat oven to 350°F. Cut slit in top of each potato; place on cookie sheet. Bake 35 to 45 minutes or until tender. Cool slightly.
3. Meanwhile, drain cod. Press with paper towels to remove excess moisture. Remove and discard skin and membranes. Finely chop cod; set aside.
4. Cut small slice off top of each baked potato. With melon baller or small grapefruit knife, scoop out each potato, leaving 1/4-inch shell. Set shells aside; reserve scooped out potato for another use.
5. Place oven rack 5 inches from broiler; heat broiler. In small bowl, combine cod, anchovies and aïoli; mix well. Fill each potato shell with about 1 tablespoon cod mixture. Place on cookie sheet.
6. Broil about 4 minutes or until lightly browned. If desired, keep warm in 200°F. oven for up to 20 minutes.*

*Can also be prepared ahead and warmed for serving.

16 tapas

Great smooth texture of potato against the crispy, salty cod.

# *Escalivada*

## Catalan Roasted Eggplant and Peppers

6 large red bell peppers

2 medium eggplants

1 medium onion, chopped

1/2 cup black olives (such as kalamata or oil-cured)

1 (2 to 2 1/2-oz.) can anchovies, drained

Extra virgin olive oil

Salt

French bread, sliced

1. Heat oven to 400°F. Place bell peppers and eggplants in shallow baking pan. Bake peppers about 35 minutes or until skin just begins to blacken, turning once. Bake eggplants about 45 minutes or until softened, turning once.
2. Place peppers and eggplants in plastic bags and seal, or cover with towel. Let stand until cool enough to handle.
3. Peel peppers and eggplants. Cut eggplants into 1/2-inch-thick slices or strips; arrange on large serving platter. Cut peppers into thin strips; place on top of eggplants.
4. Sprinkle with chopped onion and olives. Arrange anchovies on top in X pattern. Drizzle with oil; sprinkle with salt. Serve with French bread.

12 servings

If you have a barbecue, the peppers and eggplants turn out even better. You can put raw onion on top, anchovies, olives, whatever you like.

Cocinero COOK

# *Patatas con Cebolla*

## Potato and Onion Salad

2 medium to large baking potatoes

2 hard-cooked eggs, peeled, cut into 1/4-inch slices

1 medium sweet onion, thinly sliced

1/4 cup extra virgin olive oil

2 tablespoons white wine vinegar

Coarse salt

1. Cook whole unpeeled potatoes in boiling salted water for 30 to 40 minutes or until easily pierced with fork. Drain; cool. Peel; cut into 1/4-inch-thick slices.
2. On large serving platter or individual salad plates, arrange potato, egg and onion slices. Drizzle with oil and vinegar. Sprinkle with salt.*

*For a little color, sprinkle with paprika, too.

4 to 6 servings

A good summer dish.

# Crema de Verduras

## Cream of Vegetable Soup

3 medium red potatoes, cut into pieces
2 medium carrots, cut into thick slices
1 stalk celery, cut into 2-inch pieces
1/2 lb. fresh spinach
3 (3/4-oz.) processed spreadable cheese wedges*
1 1/2 cups whole milk

1. Cook potatoes, carrots and celery in boiling salted water until tender. Add spinach; cook several minutes until tender. Drain.
2. Place mixture in food processor or blender. Add cheese; process. Add milk gradually; blend to desired consistency.

*Such as The Laughing Cow brand cheese wedges.

6 servings

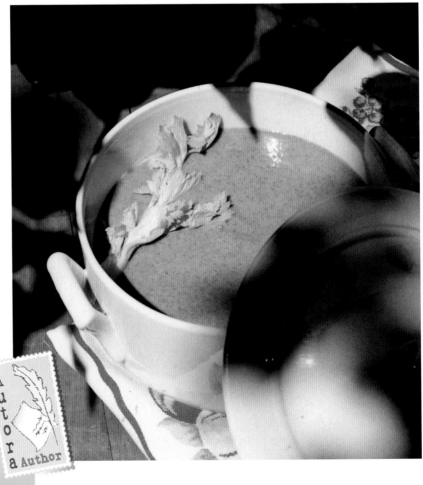

A versatile make-ahead soup that can be served hot in winter or chilled in summer. Add freshly ground pepper to taste.

Autor a Author

## *Revoltillo*

### Scrambled Eggs and Spring Vegetables
*Isabel Uroz*

"When I'm cooking, I like to do it well. I prefer not to make dishes that are very complicated, not to spend a lot of hours in the kitchen. ... My family tries to all get together at midday to eat."

*4 to 5 tablespoons olive oil*

*1 cup sliced (1/2-inch) spring garlic or garlic scapes\**

*1 lb. asparagus spears, cut into 1/2-inch pieces*

*8 oz. wild mushrooms (such as shiitake, oyster, chanterelle or a combination)*

*5 eggs*

*1 teaspoon salt*

*Freshly ground pepper*

1. Heat 2 tablespoons of the oil in large skillet over medium heat until hot. Add spring garlic; sauté about 6 minutes or until tender. Remove from skillet.
2. Add an additional tablespoon oil to skillet. Add asparagus; cook about 10 minutes or until tender, stirring occasionally. Remove from skillet.
3. Add 1 to 2 tablespoons oil to skillet. Add mushrooms; cook about 5 minutes or until softened. Stir in spring garlic and asparagus.
4. In small bowl, lightly beat eggs with salt and pepper. Pour over vegetables in skillet; cook until eggs are set, stirring occasionally.

\*Spring garlic or garlic scapes are available in the spring at farmers' markets, co-ops and some supermarkets.

4 to 5 servings

The eggs can be made with shrimp, or fish, or other things you like; with other types of mushrooms too.

# Empanada Gallega

## Galician Empanada

### Filling

1/2 lb. boneless pork chops or pork tenderloin
1/4 cup chopped red bell pepper
4 tablespoons chopped fresh parsley
3 garlic cloves, chopped
1/2 cup water
2 tablespoons olive oil
2 medium onions, chopped
2 medium tomatoes, peeled, seeded and chopped*
2 chorizos, sliced or crumbled
1/4 cup chopped prosciutto or serrano ham
2 hard-cooked eggs, peeled, chopped
Salt and freshly ground pepper

### Dough

4 cups flour
1 teaspoon baking powder
1/2 teaspoon salt
1/8 teaspoon paprika
1/2 cup olive oil
1/2 cup dry white wine
1/2 cup water
1 whole egg
1 egg, separated

1. To make filling, cut pork into small pieces; place in glass bowl or container. In food processor or with mortar and pestle, finely chop bell pepper, 2 tablespoons of the parsley and garlic. Stir in water. Pour over pork; cover and refrigerate at least 2 hours or overnight to marinate.
2. Heat 2 tablespoons oil in large skillet over medium heat until hot. Add onions; sauté until softened. Drain marinade from pork. Add pork and tomatoes to skillet; cook until pork begins to brown; reduce heat, simmer 5 minutes. Add chorizos and ham; cook until thoroughly heated, about 5 minutes. Remove from heat; drain off any remaining liquid. Stir in hard-cooked eggs and remaining 2 tablespoons parsley. Season to taste with salt and pepper.
3. To make dough, in large mixer bowl, combine flour, baking powder, salt and paprika; mix well. Add oil, wine, water, 1 egg and 1 egg white; mix until well blended.
4. Turn dough out onto floured surface; knead dough briefly until smooth, elastic and no longer sticky, adding flour if necessary. Cover; let rest 20 minutes at room temperature.
5. Heat oven to 350°F. Grease cookie sheet or 12-inch pizza pan. Divide dough in half. Pat half of dough onto greased cookie sheet. Top with filling, spreading to 1 inch from edges.

6. Shape remaining half of dough; place over filling. Bring bottom dough up over top dough; pinch well to seal. Lightly beat remaining egg yolk; paint dough with egg. In center, cut several small holes in dough to allow steam to escape.
7. Bake 25 to 30 minutes or until crust is golden brown.

*See page 35.

8 servings

# Pollo a la Buena Mujer

## The 'Good Wife's' Chicken

| | |
|---|---|
| 2 tablespoons olive oil | 1/2 cup cognac |
| 3 lb. chicken thighs | 1 1/2 chicken bouillon cubes |
| Salt and freshly ground pepper | 2 bay leaves |
| 2 large onions, sliced | |
| 2 cups freshly squeezed orange juice | |
| (about 6 medium oranges) | |

1. Heat oil in large skillet over medium-high heat until hot. Add chicken; season to taste with salt and pepper. Cook chicken 20 to 25 minutes or until browned. Remove chicken from skillet.
2. Reduce heat; add onions to same skillet. Cook about 5 minutes or until softened, stirring occasionally.
3. Stir in orange juice, cognac, bouillon cubes and bay leaves. Top with chicken. Bring to a boil. Reduce heat; simmer, uncovered, about 30 minutes or until chicken is fork-tender, its juices run clear and liquid is reduced. Remove bay leaves before serving.

4 to 6 servings

My sister-in-law gave me the recipe. It's from Andalucía. I've never seen anyone here in Catalunya make it. I take it whenever it's my turn to bring a dish. Everybody likes it a lot.

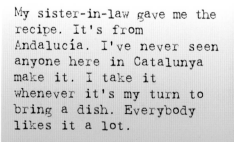

# Leche Frita

## Fried Milk

| | |
|---|---|
| *2 cups whole milk* | *1 egg, beaten* |
| *1/3 cup sugar* | *1 cup bread crumbs* |
| *1 cinnamon stick* | *Oil for frying* |
| *Peel from 1/2 lemon* | *2 tablespoons powdered sugar* |
| *1/3 cup cornstarch* | *1 1/2 teaspoons cinnamon* |
| *Flour* | |

1. In medium saucepan, bring 1 3/4 cups of the milk, sugar, cinnamon stick and lemon peel to a boil over medium heat. Reduce heat; simmer 10 minutes. Remove saucepan from heat.
2. Meanwhile, grease 8-inch square pan or 9x5-inch loaf pan. In small bowl, combine remaining 1/4 cup milk and cornstarch; blend well.
3. Slowly pour cornstarch mixture into milk mixture in saucepan. Bring to a boil, stirring constantly. Reduce heat; simmer about 2 minutes or until thickened, stirring constantly.
4. Remove and discard cinnamon stick and lemon peel. Pour into pan. Cool until steaming stops. Cover; refrigerate until custard is firm, at least 2 hours or overnight.
5. Cut custard into rectangles. Dust each with flour. Dip in beaten egg; coat with bread crumbs.
6. Heat 3/4 inch of oil in large skillet over high heat until very hot. Fry custard rectangles in hot oil until golden brown on both sides. Remove from skillet; drain on paper towels. Sprinkle with mixture of powdered sugar and cinnamon. Serve warm. If desired, keep warm in 200°F. oven for up to 30 minutes.

6 servings

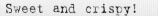

Sweet and crispy!

# Cogollos de Tudela

## Lettuce Heart Salad

*Carmen Soto*
*Restaurant Carmen, Barcelona*

"I have a good time cooking. I enjoy the relationship with the public, all that. At times I organize parties for my customers to welcome the summer. I make a tasting menu—six or seven different dishes for people to try. With the arrival of warm weather, they're more inclined to party."

*1 head Bibb lettuce, quartered*
*1 (6-oz.) can tuna in olive oil, undrained*
*1 large tomato, halved, thickly sliced*
*1/4 cup extra virgin olive oil*
*1/4 cup red wine vinegar*
*Salt and freshly ground pepper*

1. On large serving platter, arrange lettuce quarters in spokes.
2. Spoon tuna into center where lettuce quarters meet.
3. Arrange tomato slices between lettuce quarters.
4. Drizzle with oil and vinegar. Sprinkle with salt and pepper.

2 servings

A cool, refreshing salad for
a hot day.

# Queimada

## Flaming Eau de Vie

2 cups Italian grappa*
1/4 cup sugar
1/2 apple, cut into thin slices
1/2 orange, peeled, cut into thin slices
1 tablespoon coffee beans

1. In flameproof bowl, combine grappa and sugar; mix well. Add apple slices, orange slices and coffee beans.
2. To flame, spoon small amount of grappa mixture into flameproof ladle or large serving spoon. (If spoon is aluminum, hold with potholder.) Holding ladle over bowl, light mixture in ladle. Slowly pour flaming liquid into bowl; stir. Let burn for several minutes to heat entire mixture. To put out flames, place lid on bowl.
3. Serve hot queimada in small heatproof cups.

*Like the original orujo used in Spain, grappa is a strong, clear brandy distilled from the skins and seeds of grapes. Other fruit eaux-de-vie such as kirsch can also be used.

8 (1/4-cup) servings

Not for the timid.

# *Carajillo*

## Coffee with a Shot

*Very strong coffee*
*Brandy, cognac or rum*

To coffee in cups or demitasses, add a pour of brandy to taste.

2 servings

A fine, very Spanish way to mellow
a meal: a shot of brandy or rum in
your coffee.

# Salsa Romesco

## Romesco Sauce

| | |
|---|---|
| 3 medium tomatoes | 2 tablespoons blanched almonds |
| 2 tablespoons olive oil | 1 to 2 bottled spicy chiles (such as |
| 1 head garlic | guindillas or jalapeños), minced |
| 2 dried chiles (such as Spanish ñoras or | 2 tablespoons white wine vinegar or |
| New Mexico style) | sherry vinegar |
| 1/2 cup olive oil | 1/4 teaspoon salt |

1. Heat oven to 500°F. Coat tomatoes using some of the 2 tablespoons oil; place in shallow baking pan. Cut thin slice off top of garlic to expose cloves; drizzle with remaining amount from 2 tablespoons oil. Place, bottom side up, next to tomatoes in pan.
2. Bake tomatoes about 20 minutes and garlic about 30 minutes or until softened, turning each halfway through baking time. Cool both. Peel tomatoes.
3. Meanwhile, soak dried chiles in hot water for 45 minutes or until flesh can be scraped out with a spoon. Drain; remove seeds, scrape out flesh and discard skin. Set aside.
4. Heat 1/2 cup oil in medium skillet over medium heat until hot. Add almonds; sauté until golden.
5. Squeeze garlic cloves out of skins into food processor. Add tomatoes, almonds with oil from skillet, flesh from dried chiles, minced pickled chiles, vinegar and salt; process until almost smooth. Serve with grilled vegetables.*

*Also delicious with steamed vegetables, grilled fish or seafood.

Makes 1 1/2 cups

Calçots without Romesco aren't worth anything. You peel and dip them in the sauce, only the lower, most tender part. It's very amusing to eat them.

Cocinero
COOK

# Calçots

## Grilled Spring Onions

*12 to 16 large spring onions (about 1 inch in diameter)*
*About 2 tablespoons olive oil*

1. Heat grill. Brush onions with about 2 tablespoons oil. Place onions on grill; cook about 15 minutes or until charred on outside, turning once.
2. To serve, let guests peel their own onions. Dip into Romesco Sauce, p. 88, or Xató Sauce, p. 137.

3 to 4 servings

# Alcachofas a la Brasa

## Grilled Artichokes

*4 medium artichokes*
*1/2 lemon*
*Olive oil*
*Red wine vinegar*

1. Heat grill. To prepare each artichoke, cut about 1 inch off top. Discard outer leaves and cut off stem.
2. Rub cut ends of leaves with lemon half. Spread leaves; drizzle with oil. Lightly sprinkle with vinegar.
3. Place artichokes upright on hot grill. Cook until tender, about 30 minutes, or until artichokes can be pierced easily by fork.
4. Serve with Romesco Sauce, p. 88, for dipping leaves and artichoke hearts.

4 servings

A wonderful, fun dish. Even the conversation opened up during the peeling of the onions.

*Charring calçots over wood and pine cones*

Spring in Catalunya is time for the calçotada, a memorable feast, often outdoors, that features spring onions (calçots) cooked over hot coals and served with Romesco or Xató sauce. This is no dainty plateful. Diners are served mounds of calçots, from which, one by one, the charred outer layers are peeled away. The tender sweet insides are then dipped into one of the inspired, garlicky, nutty, oil-based sauces. Bibs are essential.

Calçots, however, are just the first course. They are usually followed by grilled lamb chops and dessert. A porrón (carafe with a side spout) of wine, poured from on high into the mouth, is passed around the table to make sure that everyone has enough to drink.

### Carmen Soto

*"They plant a big onion, bury it, and the shoots that it sends off are the calçots.*

*How to eat calçots*

*The onion falls apart underground and the shoots are left. They grow like leeks, but are much sweeter. In each onion there are about seven shoots. ... They only have calçots here in Catalunya. The season begins in December and ends at the end of April."*

### Isabel Uroz

*"The original menu for a calçotada was much bigger, beginning with little things to 'picar' (nibble on), such as filberts and almonds. Next came heaps of calçots to dip in Romesco sauce, followed by white beans and butifarra sausage cooked over hot coals, artichokes also prepared over hot coals, and roasted potatoes. And then, the traditional grilled lamb! There was lots of red wine, of course, and champagne. And to finish the meal, a favorite Catalan dessert, creamy sugar-glazed Crema Catalana."*

# Ensalada de Arroz

## Rice Salad

*Nacho Jiménez Uroz*

"You know, for me food is very important. Sharing it with friends is even better, above all if you try new things. You can get recipes from books, of course, but there's also cooking that goes from generation to generation. I've learned a lot from my mother, and she in turn from my grandmother."

**2 cups water**

**1/2 teaspoon salt**

**1 cup short-grain (Arborio) rice**

**2 hard-cooked eggs, peeled, chopped**

**1 medium to large tomato, chopped**

**1/2 medium onion, thinly sliced**

**2 oz. Manchego or Parmesan cheese, cubed (1/2 cup)**

**3 tablespoons extra virgin olive oil**

**Sprinkle of fresh lemon juice, if desired**

**Salt**

**6 cups torn romaine lettuce leaves**

**1/4 cup kalamata or green pimiento-stuffed olives, halved**

1. In medium saucepan, bring water and 1/2 teaspoon salt to a boil. Stir in rice; return to a boil. Reduce heat; cover and simmer 10 to 12 minutes or just until rice is done. Drain; rinse with cold water. Drain well.
2. In large bowl, combine cooked rice, eggs, tomato, onion, cheese, oil, lemon juice and salt.
3. Arrange lettuce leaves on serving platter. Spoon rice mixture over lettuce. Sprinkle with olives.

6 servings

I make things that are very easy. Uncomplicated. For example, if you have white rice already cooked you can prepare this salad in a moment. I make it a lot.

COOK

# *Patatas Rellenas de Rocafort*

## Roquefort-Stuffed Potatoes

*1 cup (4 oz.) crumbled Roquefort or blue cheese*
*1/2 cup butter, softened*
*24 small potatoes (1 1/2 to 2 inches in diameter)*
*Salt and freshly ground pepper*
*Paprika, if desired*

1. In small bowl, beat cheese and butter with mixer until smooth. Shape mixture by rounded teaspoonfuls into 24 (3/4-inch) balls; place on cookie sheet or in baking pan with sides. Cover; freeze at least 2 hours.
2. Heat oven to 350°F. Cut slit in top of each potato; place on cookie sheet. Bake 35 to 45 minutes or until tender. Cool slightly.
3. Increase oven temperature to 400°F. Cut small slice off top of each baked potato. With melon baller or small grapefruit knife, scoop out enough cooked potato from each for cheese ball to fit inside. Sprinkle potato shells with salt and pepper; reserve scooped out potato for another use.
4. Place 1 frozen cheese ball in each potato shell. Sprinkle with paprika.
5. Bake at 400°F. for 8 to 10 minutes or until cheese is melted. Serve warm. If desired, keep warm in 200°F. oven for up to 20 minutes.

24 tapas

Roasted perfectly and melty.

# Esqueixada

## Salt Cod Salad

1/2 lb. dried boneless salt cod
2 medium tomatoes, chopped
1/2 cup chopped red bell pepper
1/2 cup chopped green bell pepper
1/4 cup chopped onion
3 tablespoons extra virgin olive oil
Salt, if desired

1. Cover salt cod with cold water; refrigerate 24 hours, changing water 4 times.
2. Drain cod. Press with paper towels to remove excess moisture. Remove and discard skin and membranes. Cut cod into 1/2-inch pieces.
3. In medium bowl, combine cod, tomatoes, red and green bell pepper, onion and oil. Sprinkle with salt. Spoon onto platter. Serve immediately.

4 to 6 servings

A color and texture extravaganza with individual flavors that blend beautifully.

Taster

# Salsa de Piñones

## Pine Nut Sauce for Pasta

*12 oz. pasta*

*1 or 2 garlic cloves, chopped*

*1/2 teaspoon salt*

*1/2 cup pine nuts, toasted*

*6 tablespoons coarsely chopped fresh parsley*

*1/2 cup grated Parmesan cheese*

*3 to 4 tablespoons extra virgin olive oil*

1. In food processor, blender or with mortar and pestle, finely chop garlic and salt. Add pine nuts and parsley; chop.
2. Add cheese and enough oil to make a thick sauce.
3. Meanwhile, cook pasta according to package directions, or until it is al dente.
4. Drain pasta; return to saucepot. Stir in pine nut sauce; serve at once.

4 servings

This is a great sauce for large-size pasta—cavatappi, penne or macaroni. Serve with extra grated cheese.

# *Pimientos a la Brasa*

## Roasted Peppers

*Lara Sacco*

"What I mainly cook are Italian recipes, but I've also learned to make the Spanish dishes I like. What I want to learn now is presentation, how to mix flavors. It's not from my mother that I know how to cook, it's from books. But, if I have doubts about something, then, yes, I send her an e-mail and she helps me. ... I love to cook. I love to invite people who like to eat and who like to try new things."

*6 medium to large red, green, orange and/or yellow bell peppers*
*4 to 6 garlic cloves, coarsely chopped*
*1/2 teaspoon salt*
*1/4 teaspoon freshly ground pepper, or to taste*
*1 to 2 cups extra virgin olive oil*
*French or Italian bread*

1. Roast bell peppers either on gas stove top or under broiler until skins are blackened. Place in plastic bag and seal, or cover with towel. Let stand until cool enough to handle. Peel off blackened skin from peppers.
2. Cut peppers into 3/8-inch strips. Place in 2-quart shallow casserole. Sprinkle with garlic, salt and pepper. Pour enough olive oil over pepper mixture to cover; stir gently. Cover; refrigerate at least 8 hours.
3. To serve, bring to room temperature. Serve with bread.

6 to 8 servings

If there's oil left over use it for salad. The garlic-flavored oil is good for grilling or roasting vegetables too.

Autora Author

# Penne con Salsa de Nueces

## Penne with Walnut Sauce

*1 lb. tricolored penne pasta*
*1/2 cup walnuts*
*1/2 cup grated Manchego or Parmesan cheese*
*1/3 cup extra virgin olive oil*
*1/2 teaspoon salt*
*2 garlic cloves, peeled*

1. In food processor or blender, process walnuts, cheese, oil, salt and garlic until fairly smooth.
2. Meanwhile, cook penne according to package directions, or until it is al dente.
3. Drain penne; return to saucepot. Stir in walnut sauce; serve at once.

4 to 6 servings

I prefer using nuts
in the shell because
sometimes shelled nuts
are a little hard. If
there's extra pasta,
cool it with cold water
and keep it to make
salad-with tomato, tuna,
olives, onion, oil, salt
and fresh basil leaf.

Cocinero
COOK

# *Salsa de Aceitunas*

## Black Olive Sauce for Pasta

*1 lb. pasta*
*1 cup black olives (such as kalamata), pitted, chopped*
*4 teaspoons capers*
*2 garlic cloves, chopped*
*1/4 cup extra virgin olive oil*

1. In food processor or blender, finely chop olives, capers and garlic. Slowly add oil, processing until well blended.
2. Meanwhile, cook pasta according to package directions, or until it is al dente.
3. Drain pasta, return to saucepot. Add olive sauce; toss to mix; serve at once.

4 to 6 servings

Use leftover sauce on toast or crackers as a savory tapa.

# Trucha al Horno

## Oven-Baked Trout

| | |
|---|---|
| *4 whole trout (about 3/4-lb. each), cleaned, scaled and heads left on* | *1 tablespoon capers* |
| *Foil* | *1/2 teaspoon salt* |
| *2 garlic cloves, chopped* | *1/4 teaspoon pepper* |
| *2 tablespoons chopped fresh parsley* | *Salt and freshly ground pepper* |
| | *2 tablespoons olive oil* |

1. Heat oven to 450°F. Rinse trout; pat dry. Cut 4 sheets of foil several inches longer than fish. Place 1 trout in center of each foil sheet.
2. Mix together garlic, parsley, capers, salt and pepper; fill trout cavities. Lightly sprinkle outsides of trout with salt and pepper. Drizzle with oil.
3. Seal packets with double-fold seals, allow room for heat expansion. Place packets in large baking dish or on cookie sheet.
4. Bake 15 to 20 minutes or until fish flakes easily with fork. Test for doneness by inserting an instant-read thermometer into thickest part of fish. Fish is done when temperature is 140°F. If it has not reached 140°F., return fish to oven and watch carefully since temperature will rise quickly.

4 servings

I'm beginning to buy fish that perhaps isn't cleaned yet, and to ask what I have to clean and how to do it. At first I was a little squeamish, but then I thought okay, if I have to do it, why not do it all?

# Fruta y Vino

## Summer Fruit in Wine

3 peaches
1 pint (2 cups) strawberries
1/2 cup dry red wine
2 tablespoons sugar

1. Drop peaches into saucepan of boiling water for 1 minute. With slotted spoon, remove peaches from water. Slip off peel. Halve peaches; remove and discard pits. Slice peaches into serving bowl.
2. Halve strawberries; add to serving bowl.
3. Combine wine and sugar; pour over fruit. Refrigerate at least 2 hours before serving.

4 servings

So good I could have
eaten six helpings.

Taste!

# Rollitos de Pollo

## Chicken Rolled with Ham and Cheese

*Carmen Mora*

"What happens is that I'm always improvising. My recipes are very homestyle and very invented."

| | |
|---|---|
| 2 boneless, skinless whole chicken breasts, flattened, halved | Salt and freshly ground pepper |
| 4 thin slices deli-smoked ham | Oil |
| 4 thin slices cheese such as Swiss or mozzarella | 1 medium onion, sliced |
| | 1/4 cup olive oil |
| | 1/4 cup dry white wine |

1. Heat oven to 350°F. Place slice of ham and cheese on each flattened chicken breast half. Roll up; secure with toothpicks. Season to taste with salt and pepper.
2. Lightly coat bottom of 2-quart baking dish with oil. Spread onion slices over bottom of dish. Top with chicken rolls. Drizzle with 1/4 cup olive oil. Cover with foil.
3. Bake 10 minutes. Uncover baking dish; drizzle with wine. Bake, uncovered, an additional 15 to 20 minutes or until chicken is no longer pink. If desired, broil several minutes until golden.

4 servings

Cocinero COOK

Let the rolls cook till they're golden brown but still juicy.

# Huevos al Nido

## Eggs in a Nest

*Fermín Sánchez Carracedo*

"Yes, yes, I love to cook. Midweek I can't because I don't have time, but on the weekend I try to take care of myself a little more. For example, I like to make meat in the oven, or fish in the microwave. Fish cooked with vegetables in the microwave, in an earthenware bowl, turns out delicious. And, it's very, very quick."

*4 large rolls (such as Vienna, kaiser or challah)\**
*4 eggs, separated*
*1/2 teaspoon salt*
*Oil for frying*

1. Cut opening in center of each roll; scoop out enough bread to make room for 1 egg yolk. Discard top part of roll.
2. Carefully place 1 egg yolk in each roll.
3. In small bowl, beat egg whites and salt until stiff but not dry. With large spoon, cover each roll with egg whites, forming mounds about 2 inches high in the center.
4. Heat 1/2 inch of oil in large skillet over medium-high heat until hot. Carefully place rolls in hot oil. With large spoon, spoon oil over top of egg whites, letting excess oil run down into skillet. Continue for 3 to 4 minutes or until whites are puffed and golden.
5. Place rolls on paper towels to drain. Serve immediately.

\*Do not use hamburger buns; they are too soft.

4 servings

This a recipe my mother taught me. It seems to be Catalan. A cook with whom she worked taught it to her some 30 or 35 years ago. Since I was small I've eaten it a lot. There's a trick to eating it. The best way is to move part of the white and dig into the yolk, and, with the knife, open the roll so that the egg spreads through it.

# Tapas

Tapas bar and restaurant, Barcelona

*Dídac López Amat*
*Estrella de Plata, Tapas; Barcelona*

"There are a lot of theories about tapas. It is said that tapas were born among the troops of King Carlos III, in the 18th century. The king was tired of the soldiers getting drunk in the wine cellars, so he mandated that a cover, or 'tapa,' of cheese or ham be put on top of the wine barrels so the soldiers would eat while they drank. If you eat you get a little less drunk. Well, that's the theory.

Tapas are very, very Mediterranean. In Greece they also like to eat small things. But more than being about regions, eating tapas is a question of climate. In summer, when it's 30° or 40°C. (about 85° to 105°F.) you're not capable of sitting down and eating a first course, a second course, dessert and coffee. But, if you're hungry, and you go from bar to bar drinking a little beer here, eating a little something there, it's another story. It's more refreshing, no?

In Greece you go and eat dolmades or you eat tsatsiki, or you eat souvlaki—those are tapas. Here they like to take a break at the noon hour and the break isn't coffee. It's a glass of wine, some tapas. It's a way of life.

In our bar, there have always been tapas. But before, you made a casserole, you served less and that was a tapa. Now they're made at the moment, one by one. Tapas aren't as common here in Barcelona. In the north there's more of a tradition."

Sausage with roasted peppers, Restaurant Alkatene, Berango

# Brandada con Pimientos

## Cod Spread with Roasted Peppers

*Sara Jiménez Uroz*

"It's not that my mother was teaching this and that. I liked it, so she didn't have to. Since I was little I've known a lot of things, from soup to rice, croquettes to meats. ... I make adaptations of my husband's cooking, from the Congo. It isn't exactly the food from there; that's not possible. At the beginning Henri found the flavor of olive oil strange. He was accustomed to Belgian cooking—butter, butter, butter. He has a little of both cultures."

---

*1 cup Brandada de Bacalao (Cod Spread), page 145*

*8 (3/8-inch-thick) slices baguette*

*Roasted red bell pepper slices\**

---

1. Spread about 2 tablespoons cod spread on each bread slice.
2. Top each with roasted pepper slices.

\*If using bottled peppers, drain well and dry on paper towels.

8 tapas

You can also fill piquillo peppers with Brandada. Top with tomato sauce and warm them a little in the oven. Brandada is a Basque dish.

# Tapa Mediterránea

## Mozzarella and Tomato Tapa

8 (3/8-inch-thick) slices baguette

Extra virgin olive oil

Coarse salt

8 thin slices plain soft white cheese (such as fresh mozzarella or queso blanco),
  cut to fit baguette slices

4 thin slices tomato, halved

1. Heat broiler or grill. Place baguette slices on cookie sheet or directly on grill. Broil or grill until toasted.
2. Drizzle a small amount of oil on each toasted baguette slice. Sprinkle with salt. Top each with 1 cheese slice and 1 half-slice of tomato.

8 tapas

Simple elegance for the height of the tomato season.

# Tapa de Camarón y Aguacate

## Shrimp and Avocado Tapa

8 (3/8-inch-thick) slices baguette
Extra virgin olive oil
1/2 lb. cooked medium shrimp, shelled
1 avocado, peeled, pitted and sliced
1/4 cup ketchup
1/4 cup mayonnaise

1. Heat broiler. Place bread slices on cookie sheet. Brush each with oil. Broil until top sides are golden brown.*
2. Arrange shrimp and avocado on each bread slice.
3. Combine ketchup and mayonnaise; drizzle over shrimp and avocado.
*Bread can also be served untoasted.

8 tapas

Beautiful sauce, velvety with
the avocado and shrimp—all
the flavors come through.

# Rabo de Toro

## Oxtails Congolese

| | |
|---|---|
| 1 (3 1/2 to 4-lb.) oxtail,* cut into 2-inch rounds | 1 bay leaf |
| Water | 2 tablespoons olive oil |
| 1 cup dry white wine | 1 medium onion, chopped |
| 2 teaspoons salt | 1 medium tomato, peeled, chopped** |
| 3 garlic cloves, peeled | 2 garlic cloves, chopped |
| 8 peppercorns | 4 teaspoons Worcestershire sauce |

1. Trim fat from oxtail rounds. Place in large deep saucepan or Dutch oven; add enough water to barely cover. Add wine, salt, 3 garlic cloves, peppercorns and bay leaf. Bring to a boil. Skim off foam; cover and simmer 2 1/2 to 3 hours or until meat is tender.
2. Heat oil in large skillet over medium heat until hot. Add onion, tomato and 2 garlic cloves; cook slowly until softened.
3. Add oxtail rounds, 3 cups broth from saucepan and Worcestershire sauce to skillet. Simmer, uncovered, 30 minutes, turning meat occasionally. If necessary, skim off excess oil from top.

*A flavorful cut of meat from a beef or veal tail; used for soups and stews
**See page 35.

4 to 6 servings

They make this dish in the Congo with water buffalo. I use bull meat. Here in the Boqueria Market you can find bull meat in the summer from the bullfights, and during the winter, well, there are the bulls that don't go to the bullfights. I use the tail of the bull. It has a lot of bones and makes a flavorful sauce. Or, I use stew meat, the part of the leg with tendons. Sometimes I add a pour of Worcestershire, which seems like a lie, but they use it a lot. This recipe is a mix of cuisines.

*Tied tomatoes are dried for winter use.*

# Mató con Anchoas

## Ricotta with Anchovies

Didac López Amat
Estrella de Plata, Tapas; Barcelona

"Let's begin in the north, in the Pyrenees. Food there is heartier, more satisfying—cooked dishes, warmer things, more sauces. As we move farther south, to Tarragona, cooking becomes a little more spontaneous, with dishes more 'of the moment,' more salads, more fresh things. Even further south you get to Andalucía—fresh gazpachos, fried fish, shrimp. ... We're talking about Catalunya, but we can say the same about Basque Country, about Galicia, too."

*8 tablespoons ricotta cheese*

*8 (3/8-inch-thick) slices baguette*

*8 anchovies*

*Extra virgin olive oil*

*Freshly ground pepper*

1. Spread 1 tablespoon cheese on each baguette slice. Top each with 1 anchovy.
2. Drizzle each with oil. Sprinkle with pepper.

8 tapas

Salted fish, Tenerife

Everybody here eats anchovies with tomatoes, and they eat the cheese (mató) with honey or with sugar. So we take mató and we take anchovies and put them together. It's delicious. They are flavors that were never thought of together.

# Manchego con Olivas Negras

## Manchego with Black Olives

Black olives (such as kalamata)
Manchego cheese, cubed

Serve olives and cheese with toothpicks as a very easy and tasty tapa.

Yum, yum, yum!

# Tripa Picante

## Spicy Tripe Stew

| | |
|---|---|
| 1 cup dried garbanzo beans | 2 tablespoons chopped, bottled spicy |
| 1 lb. beef tripe | chiles (such as quindillas or jalapeños) |
| 2 tablespoons olive oil | 1 teaspoon salt |
| 1 medium onion, chopped | 1/2 teaspoon paprika |
| 2 medium tomatoes, chopped | 1/2 teaspoon dried thyme |
| 1 medium green bell pepper, chopped | 1 bay leaf |
| 1 medium red bell pepper, chopped | Dash red pepper flakes |
| 2 garlic cloves, chopped | 2 cups water |
| 2 tablespoons chopped fresh parsley | 2 medium chorizos, sliced |

1. Soak beans overnight in water to cover. Drain just before using.
2. Wash tripe thoroughly. Place in pot of boiling water to cover. Drain immediately; cool.
3. Heat oil in large saucepot or Dutch oven over medium heat until hot. Add onion; sauté until softened. Add tomatoes, green and red bell peppers, garlic, parsley, chiles, salt, paprika, thyme, bay leaf and red pepper flakes; sauté slowly until vegetables are softened.
4. Cut tripe into 1-inch strips, then into bite-sized pieces. Add to saucepot; add water. Bring to a boil. Reduce heat; cover and simmer 1 1/2 hours.
5. Add drained beans to saucepot. If necessary, add extra water. Simmer 1 hour or until tripe and beans are tender, adding chorizo during last 15 minutes of cooking. Remove bay leaf before serving.

4 to 6 servings

This dish is very gelatinous; it keeps on cooking and getting thicker. It's eaten with at least a little spice. Not like in Mexico where there is a culture of eating spicy food, but yes, a little spicy. When you make something like this, you say you're making a dish that calls for wine, 'llama al vino.' Because of the spiciness, it invites the wine.

Cocinero
COOK

# *Mejillones*

## Steamed Mussels

| | |
|---|---|
| *1 lb. mussels* | *1 small tomato, halved, grated* |
| | *1 garlic clove, chopped* |
| **Sofrito** | *1 bay leaf* |
| *2 tablespoons olive oil* | *2/3 cup dry white wine* |
| *1/2 medium onion, chopped* | |
| *1 medium carrot, chopped* | |

1. Scrub mussels thoroughly under cold running water; remove beards from between shells.
2. Heat oil in large skillet over medium heat until hot. Add onion, carrot, tomato, garlic and bay leaf; cook until vegetables are softened, stirring occasionally.
3. Add mussels and wine; cover and cook 5 minutes. Uncover; stir and continue cooking until all mussels have opened. Discard any that do not open. Remove bay leaf.
4. Divide mussels into individual bowls. Pour sauce over mussels. Serve with crusty French bread for dunking into sauce.

4 servings

Light, pure, lets the flavor of the mussels come through.

# Espárragos a la Parrilla

## Broiled Asparagus

*1 lb. asparagus spears*
*1 tablespoon olive oil*
*1 teaspoon balsamic vinegar*
*Coarse salt*

1. Heat broiler. Lightly coat baking pan with olive oil. Arrange asparagus spears in single layer in pan. Drizzle with oil; turn to coat all sides.
2. Broil 4 to 6 inches from heat for 2 to 3 minutes. Turn spears; broil an additional 2 to 3 minutes or until tender.
3. Place asparagus spears on serving platter. Drizzle with vinegar. Sprinkle with salt.

4 servings

Couldn't be better.

Taster

# Pato con Peras

## Duck with Pears

| | |
|---|---|
| 1 to 2 tablespoons olive oil | 4 medium tomatoes halved, grated |
| 1 (4 to 5-lb.) duck, cut into pieces | 1 teaspoon salt |
| Salt and freshly ground pepper | 1 teaspoon fresh thyme leaves or |
| 3 firm pears (such as Bosc or Anjou), |   1/2 teaspoon dried |
|   peeled, cored and cut into 1-inch slices | 1/4 teaspoon freshly ground pepper |
| 1 large onion, chopped | 1 bay leaf |
| 4 garlic cloves, finely chopped | |

1. Heat oil in large skillet over medium-high heat until hot. Add duck; season to taste with salt and pepper. Cook 20 to 25 minutes or until duck is browned. Remove duck from skillet; place in large saucepot or Dutch oven. Reserve 2 tablespoons drippings; discard rest.
2. In same skillet, combine pears and reserved drippings; reduce heat to medium; cook about 2 minutes or until small brown spots appear but pears are still firm. Remove pears from skillet; set aside.
3. Add onion to same skillet; cook about 10 minutes or until well browned, stirring occasionally.
4. Add garlic; cook 1 minute. Add tomatoes, 1 teaspoon salt, thyme, pepper and bay leaf; reduce heat; cook 5 to 10 minutes or until slightly reduced.
5. Pour tomato mixture over duck in saucepot. Bring to a boil. Reduce heat; cover and simmer 40 minutes.
6. Gently stir in pears; cover and cook 15 to 20 minutes or until pears and duck are tender. Remove bay leaf before serving.

6 servings

A classic dish from northern Catalunya, the region of the Empordá. ... To make a traditional Sofrito, cut the onion very small, heat it slowly, slowly, slowly until it takes on a nice browned color, then add the tomato and let it cook until it loses all the liquid and all the acidity. You can rectify it if you want with a little sugar. Add bay leaf, a little thyme, some garlic cloves and let it turn into a jam, like marmalade. Okay? A sofrito needs an hour. You can do it more quickly if you want, but the best is little by little until it turns into a jam.

Onion braids: Market, Santiago de Compostela

# Pan y Chocolate

## Bread and Chocolate Tapa

10 (3/8-inch-thick) slices baguette
Extra virgin olive oil
Coarse salt
1 (3-oz.) bar Swiss bittersweet chocolate

1. Heat broiler. Place bread slices on cookie sheet. Broil until toasted.
2. Heat oven to 350°F. On cookie sheet, drizzle each baguette slice with oil. Sprinkle each with salt. Place 2 small rectangular sections of chocolate on top of each slice.
3. Bake 5 minutes or until chocolate is melted. Serve warm.

10 tapas

Everything in La Estrella is born from popular culture, not just invented a few hours ago. There aren't dramatic or abrupt changes; it's an evolution of a way of eating.

## Catalan Architecture

-Cross the river and enter the past.... Girona has a beautiful, well-preserved medieval section, a treasure trove of Gothic and Romanesque art and an interesting Jewish quarter. It is considered one of the best places to live in Spain.
- Contrasting the earth colors of northern Catalunya and the Costa Brava, Cadaqués is all gleaming white houses with red tile roofs. Charming ... and full of tourists.
- Tarragona is a Roman city, once the center of all Iberia. There are still ruins there and a wonderful museum full of Roman artifacts.
- You can experience Modernisme in all its forms in Barcelona. The Ruta de Modernisme includes 50 architectural jewels, from parks, palaces, facades, interiors and rooftops, to Gaudí's unfinished masterpiece, La Sagrada Família.

*Crossing the river, Riu Onyar, Girona*
*La Sagrada Família, Antoni Gaudí, Barcelona (top of page)*

# *Habas a la Catalana*

## Catalan Fava Beans

*Manuel Casanovas*

"In the farmers' markets, the produce is usually fresher. There are stands where the farmers sell things directly from the country, but every day there are fewer. And you have to know the farmers. The ones I know speak to me in code, 'You bought that yesterday, so buy this one today.' They're telling me which one is better without having other people think something is bad."

| | |
|---|---|
| 1 tablespoon olive oil | 2 tablespoons chopped fresh mint leaves |
| 2 oz. salt pork, cut into small pieces | or 1 teaspoon dried mint flakes |
| 1 medium onion, chopped | 1 teaspoon salt |
| 1 lb. frozen fava beans or lima beans | 1 cup water |
| 1 small tomato, peeled, chopped* | 1 (6-inch) piece blood sausage, cut into |
| 1 garlic clove, unpeeled | serving pieces** |

1. Heat oil in medium saucepan over medium heat until hot. Add salt pork; sauté until browned. Remove salt pork from saucepan; set aside.
2. Add onion to same saucepan; sauté until golden. Add fava beans, tomato, garlic, mint, salt, reserved salt pork and water. Bring to a boil. Reduce heat to low; simmer about 15 minutes or until beans are tender.
3. Just before beans are done, add sausage; cook about 5 minutes.

*See page 35.

**Blood sausage can be found in specialty food or meat markets.

4 to 6 servings

In the country there's mint planted all over. Here no. When we're in Barcelona, we use the dried. ... This dish can be made with any blood sausage. What you have to do is not let it cook very long or it will fall apart.

COCINERO
COOK

# Setas

## Wild Mushroom Sauté

2 tablespoons olive oil

8 oz. wild mushrooms (such as shiitake, crimini, oyster or a combination)*

1 garlic clove, chopped

1 to 2 tablespoons chopped fresh parsley

1. Heat oil in skillet over medium heat until hot; add mushrooms and garlic; sauté until tender. Or, place on lightly oiled foil and cook over hot coals.
2. Sprinkle mushrooms and garlic with parsley. Serve in small bowls as a tapa or side dish.

*Wild mushrooms can also be combined with domestic mushrooms.

2 to 3 servings

The way mushrooms should be served.

# Membrillo al Horno

## Baked Quince

*Fresh quince (1/2 quince per person)*
*Whipping cream, if desired*

1. Heat oven to 350°F. Wash quince; lightly prick skin with fork in a few places.* Place on cookie sheet.
2. Bake 40 to 50 minutes or until quince is tender when pierced with fork or tip of knife. Serve warm or cold, sliced or cut into quarters. Top with sweetened whipped cream, if desired.

*Prick on bottom for best appearance.

This is traditionally served along with baked sweet potatoes.

# Almendras Garrapiñadas

## Caramelized Almonds

*4 oz. (3/4 cup) whole almonds with skins*
*3/4 cup sugar*
*3/4 cup water*

1. Line cookie sheet with foil; grease foil.
2. In large skillet, combine almonds, sugar and water. Bring to a boil over high heat, stirring constantly with wooden spoon until almonds are toasted and sugar crystallizes.
3. Immediately spread mixture on lined cookie sheet, separating into individual sugar-coated almonds. Cool.

Makes 2 cups

These are fabulous, crispy, crunchy almonds.

# Ensalada Catalana

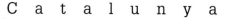

## Catalan Salad

*Josefina Pagès*

"When I cook, I put two or three dishes in the oven—one with a slice of pork loin, one with veal, whatever. Then I look for the chickens for the week and put them in the same oven, and I have two or three meals ready. It's possible to make a lot, freeze half and there you are."

| | |
|---|---|
| 1/3 cup red wine vinegar | 6 radishes, made into flowers |
| 1/3 cup water | 1/3 cup black and green olives |
| 6 green onions, cut into | 1 tablespoon capers |
| 1/2-inch slices | 6 tablespoons extra virgin olive oil |
| 6 cups torn lettuce | or to taste |
| 1 medium red bell pepper, | 2 tablespoons red wine vinegar or |
| thinly sliced | to taste |
| 1 medium tomato, thinly sliced | Salt |
| 1 medium carrot, grated | |

1. In small bowl, combine 1/3 cup red wine vinegar and water. Add green onions; let soak 15 to 30 minutes. Drain; set onions aside.

2. Arrange lettuce on very large serving platter. Top with bell pepper, tomato, green onions, carrot, radish flowers, olives and capers.

3. Drizzle salad with oil and vinegar. Sprinkle with salt. Serve immediately.

6 servings

This is served on a big platter, depending how many diners there are, and placed in the center of the table. Each person eats what he or she wants right from the platter.

# Mar i Muntanya

## Sea and Mountain (Prawns and Chicken)

2 tablespoons olive oil

2 tablespoons solid shortening or lard

4 garlic cloves, peeled

10 blanched almonds or hazelnuts,
  toasted, ground*

3 to 3 1/2 lb. cut-up chicken

Salt and freshly ground pepper

3 to 4 medium tomatoes, halved, grated

1/4 cup cognac

3/4 teaspoon salt

2 oz. bittersweet chocolate, grated

6 to 8 prawns or jumbo shrimp in shells

1. Heat oil and shortening in large skillet over medium heat until shortening is melted. Add 3 of the garlic cloves; cook until browned.
2. Remove garlic from skillet; place in food processor or mortar with remaining uncooked garlic clove and almonds; process until mixture is fine.
3. Meanwhile, add chicken to same skillet; season to taste with salt and pepper. Cook chicken 20 to 25 minutes or until browned.
4. Remove chicken from skillet; place in large cazuela (a wide, shallow earthenware casserole) or Dutch oven. Add tomatoes, cognac and 3/4 teaspoon salt. Bring to a boil over medium heat. Reduce heat; simmer, uncovered, about 20 minutes or until chicken is fork-tender and juices run clear.
5. Stir in garlic/almond mixture and chocolate until well blended. Rinse prawns; pat dry. Stir in prawns; simmer 5 to 10 minutes or until prawns turn pink.

*To toast nuts, see page 232.

6 servings

The chocolate gives this dish a slightly bitter taste.

Cocinero
COOK

# *Crema Catalana*

## Catalan Custard with Burnt Sugar Topping

| | |
|---|---|
| 4 cups whole milk | 1/4 cup cornstarch |
| 1/2 cup sugar | 8 egg yolks |
| 1 vanilla bean, split, or 1 cinnamon stick | Sugar |
| Peel from 1 lemon | |

1. In medium saucepan, bring 3 2/3 cups of the milk, 1/2 cup sugar, vanilla bean and lemon peel to a boil over medium heat. Remove from heat. Remove vanilla bean; scrape seeds from center into mixture. Remove lemon peel.
2. Add cornstarch to remaining 1/3 cup milk; blend well. Add to hot milk mixture. Stir in egg yolks. Cook over medium heat about 5 minutes or until mixture begins to thicken, stirring constantly.
3. Pour into individual dessert dishes, typically flat earthenware bowls. Cool. Refrigerate until serving time.
4. Just before serving, sprinkle 1 tablespoon sugar evenly over each custard. To caramelize sugar, use hot "branding iron" or torch, or heat under broiler until sugar melts and turns golden brown.

8 servings

This recipe is from my grandmother. I make it a lot. It's very typical, very Catalan. If you want it to be yellower, put in more egg yolks.

# Guisantes al Tuntún

## Peas 'Without Thinking'

*Dinorah Brun*

"I'm so busy I don't have time to cook. The important thing is for everyone to be together."

*1 tablespoon olive oil*
*1/2 cup chopped onion*
*2 oz. (1/2 cup) chopped prosciutto or*
  *serrano ham*
*1 (10-oz.) pkg. frozen peas or 2 cups*
  *fresh peas*

*2 tablespoons water*
*1/2 teaspoon garlic salt*
*Salt and freshly ground pepper*

1. Heat oil in medium skillet over medium heat until hot. Add onion; sauté until it just begins to brown. Add ham; sauté 2 minutes.
2. Add peas, water and garlic salt; cover and cook 2 to 4 minutes or until peas are tender, stirring once or twice. Season to taste with salt and pepper.*

*For a creamy version, stir 1/3-1/2 cup cream into the peas. Heat until warm.

4 servings

Taster: I can honestly say, since I was seven I have not liked peas, but I had two helpings. I like that it is light, unlike most pea dishes which are buttery.

*Ferran Adrià, El Bulli*
*Chef, owner, creative force, El Bulli, Michelin 3-Star Restaurant*

"Traditional cuisine is one of the places that inspire us ... to change it, make it evolve. But ours is not based entirely on traditional cooking. The year is very long and a lot can be done. One day you can rely on traditional cooking and the next on Japanese cooking. And then, on nothing, on the food. At El Bulli we change everything each year, from the bread to the last petit four. That's the idea—it's all theater. We present a very personal show. What changes is the cooking.

To learn, I always ask 'why,' about a lot of things. Apart from this, I'm a great defender of tradition. But I think tradition has always been evolutionary. Tradition is transmission, okay? What you're writing about is what is done at home. The problem is that at home, today, they don't do that kind of cooking because there isn't time. European women no longer cook as a vocation because they work, and both they and their husbands arrive late in the evening. A lot of young people don't have a reason to cook. Tradition ... transmission are broken. What you're doing with traditional cooking is what they do in restaurants. Or on weekends.

If you brought out a book about home cooking in Europe, you'd have to write the book about frozen foods. Or about historical cooking. Yes, there are people who do cook—four with first and last name! There are still people in Spain who go home and people who cook. But young people don't cook traditional cuisine. They don't have the time required. It takes two hours to make a good fricandó (veal with sauce) ... and then to make the soup?

What happens is that we, the people who love gastronomy, in a certain way are its last guardians. The problem is that you can't save history.

# El Gazpacho Más Rapido del Mundo

## The Fastest Gazpacho in the World

*Ferran Adrià*

"The world is about time in everything. That's why fine cooking is a luxury, because when we have time it's a big day. It's unique. You can't go every day to a restaurant for five hours. You can't. If it were about price, a lot of people could go often. It's the time. When you go, you want something unique, special, more than a meal. Today gastronomy is an experience. For me gastronomy is emotion."

*4 cups coarsely chopped, seeded, peeled tomatoes (about 8 medium)\**

*2 cups cubed seeded watermelon*

*1 tablespoon extra virgin olive oil*

*1 teaspoon chopped fresh basil*

*1/2 teaspoon salt*

1. Combine half of all ingredients in food processor; process until smooth.
2. Repeat with remaining half of ingredients. Refrigerate until thoroughly chilled. Serve in wine glasses.

\*See page 35.

4 to 6 servings

This is a fun recipe that you can make at home: the fastest gazpacho in the world. The important thing is the concept.

Cocinero

COOK

# Huevos Ferran

## Eggs Ferran

*1 tablespoon olive oil*
*1/4 cup chopped prosciutto or serrano ham*
*4 eggs*
*Salt and freshly ground pepper*
*1 1/2 lb. asparagus spears, roasted or steamed\**

1. Heat oil in large nonstick skillet over medium heat until hot. Add ham; sauté several minutes or until crisp. Remove ham from skillet; set aside to drain.
2. Add eggs to skillet; fry until yolks are set. Season to taste with salt and pepper.
3. Place about 6 asparagus spears on each plate. Top each with fried egg and ham.

*Asparagus can be served warm or at room temperature.

4 servings

At home I don't cook. But if I
did, it would be something fast.

# Pescado al Horno

## Baked Fish and Vegetables

*Mercé Casanovas*

"Food, cooking, eating, how many meanings, thoughts, sensations, experiences and memories are hidden behind these words! What a privilege to be able to gratify a biological necessity with an endless amount of experiences and human values like friendship, family, culture, personal identity, and so on. How wise it is that we are what we eat, how we eat, and with whom we eat!"

| | |
|---|---|
| 4 medium baking potatoes, peeled, cut into 1/8-inch-thick slices | 1 to 2 medium onions, sliced |
| Salt and freshly ground pepper | 3 to 4 medium tomatoes, sliced |
| 2 to 2 1/4 lb. (1 large or 2 small) whole fish (such as sea bass, snapper, grouper or yellow tail), cleaned, scaled and scored | 1/2 cup dry white wine |
| | 1/2 cup water |
| | 1/4 cup olive oil |
| | Lemon slices, if desired |
| 1 lemon, halved | Finely chopped parsley, if desired |

1. Heat oven to 350°F. Lightly cover bottom of large baking dish with olive oil. Arrange potato slices in bottom of baking dish. Sprinkle with salt and pepper.
2. Rinse fish; pat dry. Rub inside and out with salt and pepper. Squeeze lemon juice over top and into scores. Place fish over potatoes.
3. Cover fish with sliced onions and tomatoes. Pour wine, water and oil over fish.
4. Bake about 30 minutes or until fish flakes easily with fork. Test for doneness by inserting an instant-read thermometer into thickest part of fish. Fish is done when temperature is 140°F. If it has not reached 140°F., return fish to oven and watch carefully since temperature will rise quickly.
5. Season fish and vegetables to taste with salt and pepper. Serve garnished with lemon slices and parsley.

4 servings

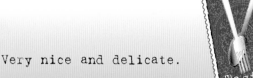

Very nice and delicate.

# Bacalao a la Catalana

## Cod with Pine Nuts and Raisins

*Roser Forn Homar*

"I've gone to cooking classes for many years. Not as a young girl, I didn't have the interest. After I was 25, 28 years old, I went to Paris to a friend's house. She had married, and I began to see what it was to cook. I began to make meals, new French dishes that Mama didn't even have any idea about. I was interested in learning, but then, later, learning more about traditional home cooking."

3 1/2 tablespoons olive oil
1/2 cup pine nuts
1/4 cup raisins
1 large onion, chopped
2 medium tomatoes, peeled, chopped*
3 tablespoons water
1/2 teaspoon salt
1 1/2 lb. cod fillets, rinsed, patted dry

Flour
Salt and freshly ground pepper
1 cup fresh or frozen peas
3 hard-cooked eggs, peeled, halved

### Picada
2 tablespoons finely chopped almonds
1 small garlic clove, finely chopped

1. Heat 1/2 tablespoon of the oil in small skillet over medium-low heat until hot. Add pine nuts and raisins; sauté until pine nuts are golden brown. Remove from skillet; set aside.
2. In same skillet, heat 1 tablespoon of the oil over medium heat until hot. Add onion; sauté until softened. Add tomatoes; sauté several minutes or until mixture becomes shiny. Add water and 1/2 teaspoon salt; bring to a boil. Reduce heat; simmer 2 minutes. Cool slightly.
3. Transfer tomato mixture to food processor or blender; process to form a smooth sauce.
4. In large skillet or paella pan, heat remaining 2 tablespoons oil over medium heat until hot. Dust cod fillets with flour; add to skillet; fry until golden. Season to taste with salt and pepper.
5. Turn fillets; top cooked side with tomato sauce. Sprinkle with pine nuts and raisins. Stir peas around fillets. Add picada of chopped almonds and garlic. Cook until fish flakes easily with fork. Serve garnished with halved eggs.

*See page 35.

6 servings

My mother always cooked and my father loved to eat! My father liked fish a lot. When his parents died he went to live with his uncles who were fish wholesalers. We ate a lot of fish at home.

Cocinero
COOK

# Sepia con Guisantes y Allioli

## Cuttlefish (or Squid) with Peas and Aïoli

| | |
|---|---|
| *1 lb. cuttlefish or squid\** | *2 medium tomatoes, peeled, seeded* |
| *2 tablespoons olive oil* | *and chopped\*\*\** |
| *1 medium onion, chopped* | *1 (1-lb.) pkg. frozen peas* |
| *1 small head garlic, cloves* | *1/2 cup water* |
| *separated, peeled\*\** | *3 tablespoons Allioli (Aïoli), page 157* |
| *Salt* | *2 hard-cooked eggs, peeled, cut into* |
| *1/2 cup dry white wine* | *wedges, if desired* |

1. Rinse cuttlefish; pat dry. Cut into 1 1/2-inch pieces.
2. Heat oil in large skillet over medium heat until hot. Add onion and garlic; sauté until softened. Add cuttlefish; season to taste with salt. Sauté until cuttlefish is opaque.
3. Add wine; bring to a boil. Reduce heat; simmer about 5 minutes.
4. Add tomatoes, peas and water. Bring to a boil. Reduce heat; cover; simmer 10 minutes or until cuttlefish is tender and peas are thoroughly heated. Serve with aïoli and egg wedges.

*See page 27.

**To peel garlic easily, lightly press clove with side of chef's knife. Peel should slip off.

***See page 35.

4 servings

Today, many innovations are made, but the base is the same. And you'll note that if you have good products, good quality foods, there's no need to add a lot of condiments.

*Daniel Rodriguez
La Bodega Pupitre,
Cooperativa Agrícola de
L'Arboç, Tarragona*

"We're an
organization of 400
families, all of
whom bring their
grapes here to the
cooperative. We have a small sparkling wine
production, some 350,000 bottles of cava (sparkling
Chardonnay) and more than 450,000 bottles of wine.

The first fermentation of cava is in the vats. Then,
when it's bottled, it goes directly to the cellar for

*Wooden pupitre*

the second
fermentation. To
be considered
sparkling wine,
cava has to spend
a minimum of 9
months in the
cellar. What
distinguishes ours
is that, at a
minimum, it's in
the cellar for 18
months and up —
36 months, 48
months. These are
the Reservas.
There are three in

*Milmanda, Fransola whites, Cellers Torres*

the Chardonnay
group from our Casa
de Pupitre that we
have in the bottle
for 36 months. We
have all the cava in
wood bottle
holders—the
'pupitres.' Every day
a man comes and
gives the bottles a
quarter turn. ... Here, we have the capacity to make a
million bottles, but we make only 350,000 a year. We're
a small winery, dedicated to producing high quality."

*Cellers Torres, Pacs del Penedès*

"We have a lot, a lot of wine, and it can't all be
bottled at once. Once it's filtered we keep it in silos
where the temperature is maintained at 6°C. (43°F.)
We have whites and rosés waiting to be bottled,
which is done within the year.

Two of our white wines are in oak: Milmanda, made
from Chardonnay grapes, and the Fransola
Sauvignon Blanc. All the reds are put in oak. Because
of the sediment, every two months the barrels are
emptied, washed with hot water, cooled and filled
again. When they are no longer used for wine, some
barrels are utilized for brandy production and can
last up to 25 or 30 years longer."

# Esqueixada de Bacallà con Salsa

## Salt Cod Salad with Tomato Sauce

*Monica Torrell Massó*

"Catalan country cooking doesn't have a major secret. It's the result of the experience of our grandmothers and the raw materials that the earth gives us."

### Esqueixada

1/2 lb. dried boneless salt cod

1 large red bell pepper

1 medium tomato, chopped

1/2 teaspoon paprika

Salt

### Salsa

2 tablespoons chopped salt cod

2 tablespoons chopped red bell pepper

2 medium tomatoes, coarsely chopped

2 anchovies, coarsely chopped

3 tablespoons extra virgin olive oil

1 tablespoon red wine vinegar

1/4 teaspoon salt

1. Cover salt cod with cold water; refrigerate 24 hours, changing water 4 times.
2. Drain cod. Press with paper towels to remove excess moisture. Remove and discard skin and membranes. Cut cod into 1/2-inch pieces; reserve 2 tablespoons for salsa. Place remaining cod in medium bowl.
3. Chop bell pepper; reserve 2 tablespoons for salsa. Place remaining bell pepper in bowl with cod. Add 1 chopped tomato and paprika; stir gently to mix. Season to taste with salt. Spoon salad onto serving platter.
4. To make salsa, in food processor or blender, process reserved cod, reserved bell pepper, and all remaining salsa ingredients until fairly smooth.
5. Pour some of salsa over top of salad. Pass remaining salsa. Serve immediately.

4 to 6 servings

Gives an original twist to a traditional recipe.

# *Pimientos de Padrón*

## Fried Summer Chiles

*Olive oil*
*1 lb. green frying chiles, small yellow banana chiles or Anaheim chiles*
*Coarse salt*

1. Heat 3/4 inch of oil in large skillet over high heat until very hot. Add whole chiles, a few at a time; fry until browned on all sides. Remove from skillet; drain on paper towels.
2. Sprinkle chiles with salt. Serve hot.

4 servings

They were darn tasty!

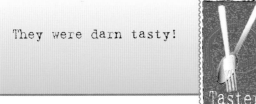

# Menja Blanc

## Cream of Almond Pudding

*Maria Dolors Massó Rovira*

"I remember making bread in the country, baking it in an oven that my grandfather built. Later on we made the dough at home and took it to the bakery to be baked. We made butifarra sausage at home, too, with pork and lamb that we bought."

| | |
|---|---|
| 1 lb. blanched almonds, finely ground | 1/4 teaspoon salt |
| 6 cups water | 1 cinnamon stick |
| 1 cup rice flour | Grated peel from 1 lemon (2 to |
| 6 tablespoons sugar | 3 teaspoons) |
| 1 tablespoon cornstarch | 1/4 teaspoon almond extract, if desired |

1. In bowl, combine ground almonds and water. Cover; refrigerate 2 hours.
2. Strain mixture through fine strainer or several layers of cheesecloth into large saucepan, pressing all liquid out of almonds. Discard almonds.
3. Stir in all remaining ingredients except almond extract. Cook over medium heat until thickened, stirring constantly. Continue cooking and stirring for 7 to 8 minutes or until no raw flour taste remains and mixture is shiny and thick.
4. Remove saucepan from heat. Cool pudding slightly. Stir in almond extract. Pour into individual small dessert dishes. Refrigerate until serving time.

6 servings

I learned to cook from my grandmother. Also, I always enjoyed it so I took an interest. Menja Blanc is served with Bunyols (donuts) for Holy Week. Or, it can be eaten alone.

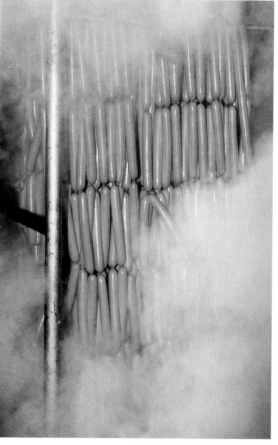

Frankfurters

Joan Baena Torres
Director, Embotits Bundó,
L'Arboç, Tarragona

"We principally make sweet ham, mortadella, frankfurters, bratwurst, and typical Catalan sausages like butifarra blanca, butifarra negra, and morcilla de cebolla. Our salted ham, or dry ham, comes both on the bone and without so it can be machine sliced. To cure a ham takes about a year. We start by covering the fresh ham with salt; the timing depends on weight. For example, a 9-10 kilogram ham (20-22 pounds) remains in salt for nine days. The salt is then rinsed off and the ham is placed in a cold chamber for 90 days. From there, it goes into a heat chamber for drying: nine months at 12° -14°C. (54-57°F.), and finally, another 15 days at 25°C. (77°F.).

In Spain, part of the cured meat is used to make bocadillos (baguette-shaped sandwiches), served plain or 'amb tomàquet' (with tomato). The rest is served as hors d'oeuvres, or as a first course with three or four types of cured meats and cheeses.

Export butifarra to the U.S.? What happens is that such things have regional boundaries. Not that they get old, but each place has a taste for particular products and the people have certain habits. For example, in Zaragosa they eat a lot of butifarra blanca. They like ours a lot but they prefer their own, perhaps for the touch they give it. Although the ingredients are the same, the spicing is different."

# Ajo de Infusión

## Steeped Garlic

*Franc Monrabà Sarrablo*
*Franc Restaurant, Barcelona*

"I want to try cooking with mud to see what happens. You take a bird, for example, feathers and all, and put it in mud, mud, mud, mud, mud. Then into the coals till the mud hardens. When the mud is broken, the feathers are stuck to it, with the skin on the bird. Many hunters did this in the woods when they hunted because they didn't have to pluck the birds. I don't have any idea how it will turn out!"

*1 cup olive oil*

*1 head garlic, separated into cloves, peeled\**

*1 cup water*

*1/2 cup white wine vinegar or sherry vinegar*

*1 teaspoon salt*

*Olives*

1. Heat oil in small saucepan over medium heat until very warm (100°F.). (This will be very warm to the touch; do not allow to boil.) Remove from heat. Add garlic cloves; cover and let stand at least 1 hour.
2. In small bowl, combine water, vinegar and salt. Strain garlic from oil.\*\* Add garlic to water and vinegar mixture. Cover; refrigerate serveral hours until chilled.
3. With slotted spoon, remove garlic from water and vinegar mixture; place in serving bowl. Add olives. Garlic mixture will keep for several days in refrigerator.

\*To peel garlic easily, lightly press clove with side of chef's knife. Peel should slip off.

\*\*Olive oil can be used in salads, for grilling or as a dip for breads.

This garlic is very simple. It's cooked by expansion which opens the pores of the food and extracts the flavor. You steep it the way you make an infusion of tea.

# Pescado con Salsa Franc

## Fish with Franc's Fresh Salsa

### Salsa
2 medium tomatoes

1 medium onion

1/2 cup extra virgin olive oil

2 tablespoons red wine vinegar

3/4 teaspoon salt

### Fish
1 1/2 to 2 lb. fish fillets (such as sea
 bass, swordfish, cod or haddock)

Flour

1 egg, beaten

Bread crumbs

2 tablespoons olive oil

1. Halve and grate tomatoes, and peel, halve and grate onion with hand grater (not food processor or blender). Stir in 1/2 cup oil, vinegar and salt. Refrigerate until ready to serve.
2. Rinse fish fillets; pat dry. Dust each fillet with flour; dip in beaten egg. Coat with bread crumbs.
3. Heat 2 tablespoons oil in large skillet over medium heat until hot. Add fish; fry several minutes on each side or until fish flakes easily with fork. Serve with salsa.

4 to 5 servings

Here's something quick and easy. The sauce depends a little on the fish. If you use 'blue' fish (sardines, anchovies, mackerel), you need a little more vinegar because they're stronger. With sea bass or swordfish or hake, which are blander, you don't need as much. ... Cooking has the benefit of making you relax a lot. You think of nothing other than applying yourself to the task. All the rest goes away.

Cocinero

COOK

# Huevos Estrellados

## Scrambled Eggs with Sausage and Potatoes

*2 tablespoons olive oil*
*2 medium red potatoes, thinly sliced*
*1/2 lb. Italian or other sausage, sliced*
*5 eggs*
*1/2 teaspoon salt*
*1/4 teaspoon freshly ground pepper*
*Anchovies, if desired*

1. Heat oil in large skillet over medium heat until hot. Add potatoes; fry until tender. Remove potatoes from skillet; place on paper towels to drain.
2. In same skillet, sauté sausage until browned and thoroughly cooked.
3. Return potatoes to skillet. In medium bowl, beat together eggs, salt and pepper; pour over potatoes. Do not stir for a few seconds; then, mix gently until eggs are set but moist. Garnish with anchovies. Serve from skillet.

4 servings

When what we studied changed from cooking to knowing how to cook, it was like having new affection for the foods, understanding their great variety, knowing the sensations of each dish.

# Ensalada Xató

## Escarole Salad with Cod and Tuna

*Maribel Masip Mirabent*

"I learned to cook at home. Moreover, I love to eat. My grandparents on my father's side are from the area of Lleida. My mother is from Tarragona, and I have taken a bit of my in-laws' cooking. A little from everyone, no? The Xató sauce is from Tarragona. More precisely, my mother is from Villa Rudona, and this is the sauce that's made there. Xató is very much in style."

### Salad

1/4 lb. dried boneless salt cod

1 head escarole

1 (6-oz.) can tuna in olive oil, drained

Black olives (such as kalamata or oil-cured)

### Xató Sauce

1 garlic clove, chopped

2 tablespoons chopped almonds

2 tablespoons chopped hazelnuts

3/4 cup extra virgin olive oil

1/4 cup white wine vinegar

2 teaspoons paprika

1/2 teaspoon salt

1. Cover salt cod with cold water; refrigerate 24 hours, changing water 4 times.
2. Drain cod. Press with paper towels to remove excess moisture. Remove and discard skin and membranes. Cut cod into 1/2-inch pieces.
3. To make sauce, in food processor, blender or with mortar and pestle, finely chop garlic, almonds and hazelnuts. Add oil; process until almost smooth. Add vinegar, paprika and salt; blend well.
4. Arrange escarole on serving platter or individual salad plates. Top each with salt cod and tuna pieces. Scatter olives over top. Shake sauce well before using; drizzle salad with sauce or serve separately.

4 to 6 servings

To make a delicious tapa, Caracoles con Xató (Snails with Xató Sauce), use the same sauce as a dip for cooked or canned snails.

Cocinero COOK

# Las Farinetes

## Winter Squash Purée

| | |
|---|---|
| 2 lb. winter squash, peeled, cubed* | 4 oz. salt pork or 6 slices bacon, cut into |
| Water | bite-sized pieces |
| 1/2 teaspoons salt | 1 tablespoon flour |
| 1 tablespoon plus 1 teaspoon olive oil | Salt and freshly ground pepper |

1. Place squash in large saucepan. Add enough water to barely cover; add salt. Bring to a boil. Reduce heat; cover and simmer about 15 minutes or until squash is tender.
2. Meanwhile, heat 1 tablespoon of the oil in medium skillet over medium heat until hot. Add salt pork; fry until crisp. Remove from skillet; drain on paper towels. Set aside. Reserve oil from skillet.
3. When squash is tender, remove from saucepan; cool slightly. Reserve water to make purée. Place squash in food processor or blender. Process squash; add 2 tablespoons reserved oil and enough reserved water to make a medium purée.
4. Heat remaining 1 teaspoon oil in medium skillet until hot. Stir in flour until smooth and bubbly. Add squash purée; cook until thickened, stirring constantly. Season to taste with salt.
5. Serve warm sprinkled with crisp salt pork and pepper.

*To make squash easier to peel, heat in microwave for several minutes. Cool slightly.

4 servings

Sauté the salt pork till it's nice and crispy.

Adriana Olivas
La Fageda

"At the non-profit cooperative, La Fageda, we have 150 workers—50 professionals and 100 who are mentally or physically disabled. Depending on their level of disability, we send them to work in one of our four businesses. We have a forest nursery, a gardening group that works for the municipality, the yogurt factory, and the cows that give us the milk to make the yogurt. We have 300 cows, 180 in production. They are the ones we milk every day at 5:00 a.m. and 5:00 p.m. Each cow generally gives us 30 liters of milk daily.

Every morning we take a sample of the milk to a laboratory for analysis.

Once we're sure it's okay, the milk goes directly to the plant. First it's put into a large funnel where the sugar and natural flavors are mixed in. Next it goes to pasteurization, where it's boiled for five minutes at 20°C. (68°F.) From there it's homogenized to eliminate the curds. Milk for fat-free yogurt is separated in a centrifuge, and the cream is sold to area restaurants.

After homogenization, bacteria for fermentation are added. It usually takes 1-1/2 hours to reach the proper level of acidity. From fermentation it goes into a very, very, very cold tunnel, -20°C. (-4°F.), for only 15 minutes. Otherwise it would be frozen yogurt!

If yogurt expires in the store, we bring it back, separate out the yogurt for the feed plant and recycle the containers. At home, if you've kept it in the refrigerator, nothing will happen, except that you can no longer call it yogurt. After 28 days the bacteria die and you have a dairy dessert."

# Pastel de Manzana

## Golden Apple Cake

*Consol Tonem Espadaler*

"I don't know much about cooking, but the little I have learned is from my mother. My mother is an expert, especially in meats and pastries. ... On the days I work, I'm used to making things that are very practical—salads and something on the grill. When I have time, I love to cook. Then I make great dishes and I shine. I always cook things from Catalunya."

2 eggs
3/4 cup flour
1 teaspoon baking powder
1/4 teaspoon salt
1/2 cup butter
1/3 cup sugar
1 large Golden Delicious apple
1 tablespoon sugar

1. Heat oven to 350°F. Grease and flour 9-inch tart or pie pan. Beat eggs in medium bowl. Add flour, baking powder and salt; mix well.
2. In medium saucepan, over low heat, melt butter and 1/3 cup sugar. Stir into flour mixture in bowl.
3. Peel apple; cut into thin slices.
4. Pour half of batter into tart pan. Top with half of the apple slices. Top with remaining batter; arrange remaining apple slices over top. Sprinkle with 1 tablespoon sugar.
5. Bake 25 to 30 minutes or until top is golden brown and toothpick inserted in center comes out clean. Serve warm or cold. If desired, serve with whipped cream.

8 servings

This recipe is from a friend of mine, from when we went to school together. It's from her grandmother so it has to be more than 80 years old. It's a typical Catalan recipe. The apples are the Golden variety, harvested in Ventalló, which is in the province of Girona in Catalunya. ...You should always mix it, if possible, with a wooden spoon. They're the best for cooking.

# *Sepia con Albóndigas*

## Cuttlefish (or Squid) with Meatballs

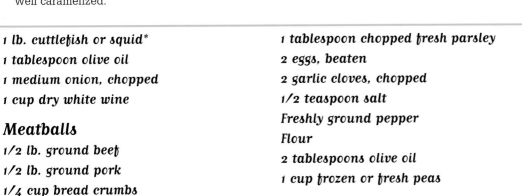

*Maria Cruz Subias*
*Montgó Sub, L'Escala*

"I've loved to cook, always, always. I learned when I was young, at home with my sisters. Also from reading, and from Quim's mother, my husband's mother. And I'm always asking: 'ay, that's good, how do you make it?' I make the best spaghettis, the best sepia with potatoes and peas, the best paellas, the best fideùas. A good sofrito is essential for the majority of the dishes, with the onion well caramelized."

| | |
|---|---|
| 1 lb. cuttlefish or squid* | 1 tablespoon chopped fresh parsley |
| 1 tablespoon olive oil | 2 eggs, beaten |
| 1 medium onion, chopped | 2 garlic cloves, chopped |
| 1 cup dry white wine | 1/2 teaspoon salt |
| | Freshly ground pepper |
| **Meatballs** | Flour |
| 1/2 lb. ground beef | 2 tablespoons olive oil |
| 1/2 lb. ground pork | 1 cup frozen or fresh peas |
| 1/4 cup bread crumbs | |

1. Rinse cuttlefish; pat dry. Cut into pieces.
2. Heat 1 tablespoon oil in large skillet over medium heat until hot. Add onion; sauté until golden. Add cuttlefish; sauté until opaque. Add wine; bring to a boil. Reduce heat; cover and simmer 20 minutes.
3. Meanwhile, combine all meatball ingredients; mix well. Shape into 1 1/4-inch balls. Coat meatballs with flour.
4. Heat 2 tablespoons oil in large skillet over medium-high heat until hot. Add meatballs; sauté until well browned on all sides.
5. Add meatballs and peas to cuttlefish mixture. Bring to a boil. Reduce heat; simmer 5 to 10 minutes to combine flavors.

*See page 27.

8 servings

The meatballs are always beef and pork, half one, half the other because the flavor is much better. Nothing difficult. They're served as an hors d'oeuvre in a lot of places.

# Pastel de Pescado

## Fish Terrine

| Fish | Terrine Mixture | Salsa Rosa |
|---|---|---|
| 3/4 lb. firm white fish (such as cod, snapper or halibut) | 3 eggs, separated | 1/4 cup mayonnaise |
| 1 teaspoon salt | 3 tablespoons tomato paste | 1/4 cup ketchup |
| Freshly ground pepper | 1/2 teaspoon salt | 1 tablespoon cognac |
| 1 medium tomato, sliced | 1/4 teaspoon pepper | |
| 1 medium onion, sliced | | Lettuce leaves |
| 1/2 cup dry white wine | | Orange slices |
| 1 tablespoon olive oil | | Lemon slices |
| | | Red caviar, if desired |

1. Heat oven to 350°F. Coat bottom of baking pan with oil. Place fish in pan; sprinkle with salt and pepper. Top with tomato and onion slices. Pour wine and oil over fish.
2. Bake 30 to 40 minutes or until fish flakes easily with fork. Let stand until cool enough to handle.
3. Remove bones from fish; place fish in food processor or blender. (Discard tomato and onion.) Add egg yolks, tomato paste, 1/2 teaspoon salt and 1/4 teaspoon pepper; process until smooth. Beat egg whites until stiff; fold into fish mixture.
4. Line loaf pan with foil; grease and flour foil. Pour fish mixture into pan. Place loaf pan in larger pan of water.
5. Bake at 350°F. for 35 to 45 minutes or until firm. Remove from oven; cool in pan 10 minutes. Remove from pan. Loaf can be served warm or chilled.
6. To serve, line individual plates with lettuce. Top each with 2 thin slices fish loaf and half slice each of orange and lemon. Drizzle each with 1 tablespoon salsa rosa. Top salsa rosa with 1 teaspoon red caviar.

6 to 8 servings

Would make a great small entree.

*Mercat de la Boqueria, Barcelona*

Joaquim (Quim)
Pallàs i Seix
Montgó Sub, L' Escala

"The region we're in, L'Escala, is famous for its salted anchovies. The most important factories are here. It is the only place that has the Denominación de Origen. But using the name anchovy can't be avoided; it's the name of the fish. What it really is, is a 'boqueron,' a variety of sardine. Boquerones are made with vinegar. The same fish in salt becomes an anchovy.

In the restaurant, I make the anchovies; I don't buy them. Commercial anchovies have an expiration date of a year, but for us they're perfectly good after a year when they have some white spots, like what happens on a ham.

Today there's great demand for anchovies. So they buy a lot, keep them in the refrigerator and then they have to use a ton of tricks so the anchovies turn out good. You eat an anchovy and it tastes good, but we find it bad because it's what we call 'testa verde.' It isn't sufficiently mature, nor does it have the proper brown color.

You can make me happy if you give me an anchovy that's two years old.

You don't have to put anything in the anchovy if it hasn't been in a refrigerator. You simply clean it, bury it in coarse salt, and put something on top to weight it. When the anchovy is pressed, it lets off its juice and you get the 'brou' (broth). It's much more natural if you do it properly. For example, I get three boxes, 20 kilos each—60 kilos of anchovies, and one morning we go 'pa, pa, pa, pa, pa, pa, pa' until it's done.

Putting anchovies in oil stops the maturation process. So if you buy cans of anchovy filets in oil, you can't improve them; you can only make them worse. For us, it doesn't make sense that you open a can and you're eating anchovies. No, you buy a jar with salt, and you do what you want, when you want. You don't have to consume the whole jar. You take out the anchovies, you rinse them well, dry them, and put on a little oil. If you like, add a few drops of vinegar and a little pepper. And that's it."

# Anguilas con Ajo y Pimiento

## Eel with Garlic and Peppers

*Joaquim (Quim) Pallàs i Seix*

"I'm very, very detail oriented. Sometimes my wife says, 'I'm going to make myself a sandwich,' and she makes a sandwich. And then I say, 'I'm going to make myself one, too.' I have a lot of patience. I cut up the lettuce very fine, the pickles very small, I mash my tuna with a little mayonnaise in the mortar. I spread it on the bread, and then garnish it. And when she sees the sandwich she gets desperate, and she says, 'listen, if I'd known you were going to make a sandwich like that, I would have asked you to make one for me, too.'"

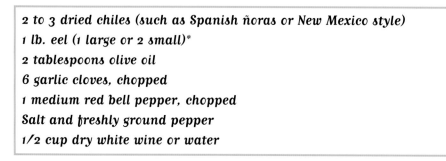

**2 to 3 dried chiles (such as Spanish ñoras or New Mexico style)**

**1 lb. eel (1 large or 2 small)***

**2 tablespoons olive oil**

**6 garlic cloves, chopped**

**1 medium red bell pepper, chopped**

**Salt and freshly ground pepper**

**1/2 cup dry white wine or water**

1. Soak dried chiles in hot water for 45 minutes or until flesh can be scraped out with a spoon. Drain; remove seeds, scrape out flesh and discard skin. Set aside.
2. Meanwhile, cut eel crosswise into strips; remove bones.
3. Heat oil in large skillet over medium heat until hot. Add garlic, bell pepper and flesh from dried chiles; sauté until softened.
4. Add eel; sauté 1 to 2 minutes or until opaque. Season to taste with salt and pepper. Add wine. Bring to a boil. Reduce heat; simmer a few minutes to blend flavors. Serve immediately.

*The most likely place to find eel is in an Asian market. It will be either fresh or frozen. If frozen, thaw in refrigerator overnight. Rinse; pat dry.

4 appetizer servings

The recipe is very easy. The most important thing is that the garlic flavor the oil. It has to change color, have this brown color, which gives a characteristic flavor to the oil. ... For this dish, it has to be red pepper; you can't use green. The flavor is completely different. The oil that's in green pepper is much stronger.

# *Brandada de Bacalao*

## Cod Spread

*1/4 lb. dried boneless salt cod*

*1 small red potato, cut into pieces (about 1/4 cup)*

*1 garlic clove, chopped*

*3 1/2 tablespoons extra virgin olive oil*

*3 tablespoons warm milk*

*Dash salt, if desired*

*Dash freshly ground pepper, if desired*

1. Cover salt cod with cold water; refrigerate 24 hours, changing water 4 times.
2. Drain cod. Press with paper towels to remove excess moisture. Remove and discard skin and membranes. Cut cod into pieces.
3. Cook potato in boiling salted water until tender. Drain.
4. In food processor or blender, process salt cod, garlic and oil. Add potato, milk, salt and pepper; process until smooth, adding extra oil and milk alternately until creamy and spreadable.

Makes 1 1/4 cups

Costa Brava, near Cadaqués

Brandada is usually made with potatoes. You mash it all together and make a paste. You can make it with spinach or with a lot of things. Milk or cream, whatever you want. Everyone has a personal style.

# *Sangría*

## Sangria

| | |
|---|---|
| *1 bottle dry red wine* | *2 peaches, sliced* |
| *1/2 cup sugar* | *1 orange, sliced* |
| *1/2 cup fresh lemon juice* | *1 lemon, sliced* |
| *1/2 cup water* | *1 cup club soda, chilled* |
| *1/4 cup brandy* | |
| *1/4 cup orange-flavored liqueur* | |
| *(such as Cointreau)* | |

1. In large pitcher, combine wine, sugar, lemon juice, water, brandy and orange-flavored liqueur; mix well. Add sliced fruit. Cover; refrigerate several hours or overnight.
2. Just before serving, add club soda. Serve very cold.

Makes 6 cups

The best sangria I've ever had. Not too sweet—lovely, subtle flavors.

España
POR AVION

Nuria and Nacho's diving friends often gather
in L'Escala at Quim's Montgó Scuba Center.
One day, when we were about to leave after a
giant midday feast, I was chatting with a
woman about cooking. She was telling me about
a traditional duck recipe that sounded
delicious. When I asked her how it was made
she said, "well, first you kill the duck."

# Valencia

The Comunitat Valenciana is made up of three provinces: Alicante, Castellón and Valencia. Of all the weeks in the year, perhaps the most eagerly awaited is when the city of Valencia celebrates its spring fire festival, Las Fallas.

There are about 800 Fallas societies in and around Valencia, and much of their work revolves around preparing for the festival. The societies hire special artists to design "fallas" for the celebration. They can range from small sculptural pieces that animate a city corner to huge constructions that take over a plaza.

*Seafood Paella. La Paz Restaurant. Valencia*

People come from far and wide to join in. There are musical groups everywhere; parades; and women in fabulous, traditional dresses of silk brocade with decorative aprons. Some sort of magic keeps their complex braided hairdos in place for the whole four-day event. And then, there is the fire itself! For three nights, Valencia treats its celebrants to jaw-dropping fireworks displays, and, by day, to a plaza full of firecrackers, set off for the sheer noise and smoke of it. On Sunday at midnight, with firemen strategically placed, the celebration ends with the burning of the fallas, all except one which is chosen to become part of history in the Fallas Museum.

Also inextricably linked to the name Valencia is paella. Though the cuisine of Valencia is influenced by what's close at hand—orange groves, vegetable gardens, an abundance of fish and shellfish, the source of its greatest culinary fame is Paella Valenciana—a dish that dates to the middle of the 19th century. Traditionally cooked outdoors over a wood fire, Paella Valenciana combines chicken, snails, fresh vegetables, and saffron with rice. But cooking good paella—and there are many variations—is more than following a recipe. It's an art to cook the rice until the exact moment when each grain is separate, dry and tender. First choice for festivals, celebrations, and special occasions, paella is enjoyed communally, with everyone eating out of the same wide shallow pan, originally called a "paella."

Many other delicious rice-based dishes await visitors to Valencia: Arròs a Banda, made with various fishes, and accompanied by garlicky **Allioli**; Arròs Negre, flavored with the ink of the cuttlefish; and oven-baked **Arròs al Forn**, originally considered too common for fine dining and now a popular restaurant dish. It is said that rice is prepared more than 100 ways in Valencia.

Other well-known Valencian dishes to try include Fideuà, similar to seafood paella but made with pasta; Pato a la Naranja, a classic recipe for orange duck; Esgarradet, a cod and red pepper combination; and finally, a soupy dish which was once the daily fare of farmers—Arròs amb Fesols i Naps, rice with white beans and turnips.

The artistry of Valencian pastry is another delight. Some examples are the Arab-inspired squash pie called Arnadí; Empanadas filled with sweet potatoes; and **Rollitos de Anís**, delicate anise-flavored cookies.

*The Virgin, made of bouquets of carnations: Las Fallas, Valencia*

In Castellón province, meat dishes are popular, especially lamb and baked kid; or hearty stews such as Castellón Olla, prepared with white beans, beef and bacon. For an unusual flavor, try the Castellón yogurt, La Collá, which is made from the pistils of wild artichokes.

Alicante province offers its own version of paella, Paella Alicantina, made with chicken and rabbit. Also, Bajoques Farcides, peppers stuffed with rice, pork, tomatoes and spices. But surely Alicante's culinary star is turrón, an almond nougat of Arab origin. It is made two ways: with whole almonds in honey and sugar (Turrón de Alicante), and with ground almonds (Turrón de Jijona).

Though you'll find the sweet refreshing drink, horchata, in other places, the real thing comes from Valencia. It is made from the bulb of the chufa (tiger nut) plant. Horchata is served very cold, and accompanied by fartons—long, thin, sweet dipping breads. Another local refresher with a loyal following is Agua de Valencia, orange juice mixed with sparkling cava wine.

To accompany a Valencian meal, try some Valencian wine, such as the light, dry whites of Albaida, Cheste and Liria; the whites from Alto Turia and Serranía; or the reds from Utiel, Campo de Liria and Requena (where a wine fountain flows, free of charge, during the grape harvest).

# *Lomo con Leche*

## Pork Loin in Milk

*Pilar Tortosa Huerta*

"Some recipes have been in our family for a lifetime. Heavens yes, for 100 years. When my mother was young, she worked as a cook in a fine house and made plates full of very good sweets, all that. Here nothing gets thrown out. If there's something left we eat it the next day. I always made extra for my husband so he could have a plate of it the following day, without heating it up or anything."

2 tablespoons olive oil
1 (3-lb.) pork loin
Salt
4 cups whole milk
1/4 teaspoon peppercorns
2 garlic cloves, crushed

1. Heat oil in large saucepot or Dutch oven over medium-high heat until hot. Add pork loin; cook 5 to 10 minutes or until browned on all sides. Season to taste with salt.
2. Add milk, peppercorns and garlic; bring to a boil. Reduce heat; cover and simmer 2 to 2 1/2 hours.
3. Remove pork loin from saucepot; place on platter. Cover to keep warm.
4. Bring milk mixture to a boil. Cook 15 minutes or until thickened, stirring occasionally. (Mixture will have a grainy, curdled appearance.) Remove from heat; cool several minutes.
5. Purée in small amounts in food processor or blender. Serve sauce over pork loin.

8 servings

Absolutely a joy to eat.

# Pierna de Ternera

## Braised Veal Shanks

| | |
|---|---|
| 2 tablespoons olive oil | 1 medium onion, sliced |
| 2 1/2 lb. veal shanks, cut onto 4 pieces | Cinnamon |
| Salt and freshly ground pepper | 4 medium red potatoes, peeled, |
| Water | quartered |
| 2 teaspoons salt | Paprika, if desired |
| 1 small head garlic, separated into cloves but not peeled | |

1. Heat oil in large saucepan or Dutch oven over medium-high heat until hot. Add veal shanks; brown on all sides. Season to taste with salt and pepper.
2. Stand shanks upright in saucepan. Add water to just cover shanks. Bring to a boil. Add 2 teaspoons salt and garlic cloves. Arrange onion slices over top of shanks; lightly sprinkle with cinnamon. Reduce heat; cover and simmer 1 hour.
3. Add potatoes to shanks. Cover; simmer 20 minutes or until potatoes and shanks are tender. Sprinkle potatoes with paprika.*

*This dish is even better reheated and served the next day.

4 servings

Deliciously tender.
Love the cinnamon.

# Paella de Pollo

## Chicken Paella

*María Carmen Borrás Tortosa*

"Here in Valencia we eat a lot of paella. For some people a portion is four tablespoons and that's enough, but for a Valencian, a portion is a big plateful. If you don't have a paella pan, use the largest frying pan you have. It's better if the pan isn't too deep."

| | |
|---|---|
| *4 tablespoons olive oil* | *3 lb. cut-up chicken* |
| *4 or 5 medium artichoke hearts or* | *Salt and freshly ground pepper* |
| *1 lb. fresh baby artichokes\** | *2 cups short-grain (Arborio) rice* |
| *1/4 lb. fresh green beans* | *6 cups water* |
| *1/2 cup frozen lima beans* | *2 teaspoons salt* |
| *1/2 cup finely chopped green bell pepper* | *1/4 teaspoon freshly ground pepper* |
| *1/2 cup finely chopped red bell pepper* | *1/4 teaspoon saffron, crumbled* |
| *1 (15.5-oz.) can large white beans, drained* | |

1. Heat 2 tablespoons of the oil in paella pan or large skillet over medium heat until hot. Add all vegetables; sauté a few minutes. Remove from pan.
2. Add remaining 2 tablespoons oil to same pan; increase heat to medium-high; heat until hot. Add chicken; brown on all sides. Season to taste with salt and pepper. Move chicken to sides of pan.
3. Stir in rice. Return vegetables to pan. Add water, 2 teaspoons salt, 1/4 teaspoon pepper and saffron. Bring to a boil. Reduce heat; simmer 15 to 20 minutes or until rice is almost done but still chewy.
4. Remove pan from heat. Cover with dish towel; let stand 5 to 10 minutes before serving to finish cooking.

*Fresh baby artichokes are available in some markets and work very well in this dish. If desired, frozen or canned artichokes can also be used.

6 to 8 servings

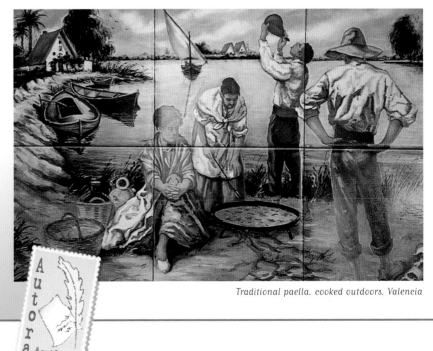

To prepare Paella del Mar (Fish and Seafood Paella), use 3 lb. mixed shrimp, clams, mussels and bite-sized chunks of firm white fish instead of chicken. Add during last 10 minutes of cooking time; cook until shrimp turn pink, clams and mussels open, and fish flakes easily with fork.

*Traditional paella, cooked outdoors, Valencia*

Autora Author

*Traslado, carrying The Virgin, patroness of Valencia*

Luckily, I was in Valencia for the annual
feast of La Virgen de los Desamparados, which
meant enjoying a weekend of traditional music
and dance and, it being Valencia, dazzling
pyrotechnics. On the day the statue of the
Virgin was carried from the cathedral, around
the plaza, through the streets and back, the
sidewalks were packed. Every so often the
carriers dipped the statue so the faithful
could touch it. People in the back began to
throw clothing forward so those up front could
touch it to the statue. When the procession
entered the final street to return to the
cathedral, the Virgin was held backwards.
She never turns her back on the people.

# Lentejas con Chorizo

## Lentil and Chorizo Stew

*Mónica Borrás*

"This can also be a vegetarian dish, without the chorizo."

| | |
|---|---|
| *4 cups water* | *2 teaspoons salt* |
| *1 cup dried lentils* | *1 bay leaf* |
| *5 garlic cloves, peeled* | *1/4 cup short-grain (Arborio) rice* |
| *3 medium to large carrots, sliced* | *1/2 lb. chorizo, sliced* |
| *1 medium red potato, cut into* | *Red wine vinegar* |
| *bite-sized pieces* | *Freshly ground pepper* |
| *1 tablespoon olive oil* | |

1. Bring water to a boil in large saucepan. Add lentils, garlic, carrots, potato, oil, salt and bay leaf. Bring to a boil. Reduce heat; cover and simmer 5 minutes.
2. Add rice; cover and simmer 15 to 20 minutes or until rice and vegetables are tender but still 'al dente.'
3. Sauté chorizo in small skillet. Add to lentil mixture toward end of cooking time. Remove bay leaf before serving.
4. Serve stew drizzled with small amount of vinegar and pepper to taste.

4 servings

Comfort food for a cold winter night.

# *Albóndigas de la Tía Dolores*

## Aunt Dolores's Meatballs

*Esther Luy*

"In this part of Valencia the food isn't very spicy. We don't use many hot peppers; it's a hot climate and spicy food makes you hot. Food follows geography. It's a cultural thing, too. In other places they'd use black pepper, but here in Valencia, we're not used to putting it in. A little, eh? But not much. We use but don't abuse."

| | |
|---|---|
| *3 eggs, slightly beaten* | *2 tablespoons chopped blanched almonds* |
| *1/2 lb. ground veal* | *2 tablespoons chopped fresh parsley* |
| *1/2 lb. ground pork* | *1 teaspoon salt* |
| *3/4 cup bread crumbs* | *Flour* |
| *4 garlic cloves, chopped* | *1 to 2 tablespoons olive oil* |

1. In medium bowl, combine eggs, veal, pork and bread crumbs; mix well.
2. In food processor or with mortar and pestle, finely chop garlic, almonds, parsley and salt. Add to meat mixture; mix well. Cover; refrigerate 2 to 3 hours.
3. Shape meat mixture into 1-inch balls. Coat lightly with flour.
4. Heat oil in large skillet over medium-high heat until hot. Add meatballs; brown on all sides. Reduce heat; cover and cook until meatballs are thoroughly cooked. Drain meatballs on paper towels. Serve with Samfaina (Vegetable Sauce), p.157.

4 servings

It's a recipe from my aunt in Zaragosa. My grandmother made them, and my mother and my aunt. ... My aunt does everything by hand. She puts the garlic and whole almonds in the mortar and 'ta, ta, ta, ta, ta, ta, ta, ta,' she keeps on mashing. ... She serves them with sautéed tomatoes, peppers and onions—what's called Samfaina here in Valencia.

*Typical Valencian mortar and pestle.*

# Samfaina

## Vegetable Sauce

| | |
|---|---|
| 2 tablespoons olive oil | 2 medium tomatoes, peeled, seeded |
| 1 medium onion, chopped | and chopped* |
| 1 medium zucchini, cubed | 1 cup chicken broth |
| 1 medium green bell pepper, chopped | Salt and freshly ground pepper |

1. Heat oil in large skillet over medium heat until hot. Add onion; sauté about 5 minutes or until softened.
2. Add zucchini, bell pepper and tomatoes; sauté about 5 minutes or until vegetables are tender.
3. Stir in chicken broth; bring to a boil. Reduce heat; simmer, uncovered, 20 to 30 minutes or until vegetables are very soft and form a sauce. If desired, stir in more chicken broth or water until of desired thickness. Season to taste with salt and pepper. Serve with meats, poultry, or as a sauce for pasta.

*See page 35.

Makes 1 1/2 cups

# Allioli

## Aïoli

| |
|---|
| 5 garlic cloves, chopped |
| 1/2 teaspoon coarse salt |
| 2 egg yolks |
| 1/2 cup extra virgin olive oil |

1. With mortar and pestle, finely mash garlic and salt. Or, put garlic through garlic press and mix with salt.
2. Place garlic mixture in blender or food processor. Add egg yolks; blend well. With motor running, slowly add oil, blending until thickened.

Makes 2/3 cup

Allioli gives a delicious bite to grilled meats, fish, seafood and rice dishes. For a quick Allioli, stir finely-chopped garlic into mayonnaise.

157

# Pescado a la Sal

## Fish Baked in Coarse Salt

> 2 (1 1/2-lb.) whole fish (such as porgy, snapper or sea bass), cleaned, scaled and
>   heads left on
> Freshly ground pepper
> Fresh thyme sprigs
> 4 cups coarse sea or kosher salt

1. Heat oven to 400°F. Lightly oil baking dish. Rinse fish; pat dry. Season with pepper. Place a few sprigs of thyme in each cavity. Arrange fish in baking dish.
2. Cover fish with salt to form 1/2-inch layer over fish.
3. Bake about 25 minutes or until fish flakes easily with fork. Test for doneness by inserting an instant-read thermometer into thickest part of fish. Fish is done when temperature is 140°F. If it has not reached 140°F., return fish to oven and watch carefully since temperature will rise quickly.
4. To serve, brush off all salt. Remove skin and discard; carefully remove bones. Arrange fish on warmed platter or individual plates. Fish will be very moist and tender. If desired, serve with a simple sauce such as Cilantro Mojo, page 209, or Mojo Verde, page 205.

4 servings

I'm sorry I'm not an expert cook,
I'm an eater!

# *Pollo a la Naranja*

## Valencia Orange Chicken

---

1/4 cup olive oil

3 to 3 1/2 lb. cut-up chicken

Salt and freshly ground pepper

4 garlic cloves, peeled

3 medium baking potatoes, peeled, cut into 1/2-inch slices

2 cups freshly squeezed orange juice (about 4 medium oranges)*

Paprika, if desired

---

1. Heat oil in large skillet over medium-high heat until hot. Add chicken; season to taste with salt and pepper. Cook chicken 20 to 25 minutes or until browned, adding garlic cloves during last minute of cooking. Remove chicken and garlic from skillet.
2. Place potatoes in large saucepot or Dutch oven; pour orange juice over potatoes. Top with chicken and garlic. Bring to a boil. Reduce heat to low; cover and simmer 15 minutes or until chicken is fork-tender and juices run clear.
3. Uncover; simmer an additional 10 to 15 minutes. For a little more color, sprinkle chicken with paprika.

*For a more intense flavor, combine 1 whole orange, cut into 8 pieces, and 1 1/2 cups fresh orange juice in blender; process until smooth.

4 servings

If you want, you can also include chopped almonds or hazelnuts in the sauce.

*Market. Santiago de Compostela*

# Pollo con Manzanas

## Chicken with Apples

*4 cooking apples (such as Granny Smith, Gala, Braeburn or Winesap),*
*unpeeled, cored and cut crosswise into 3/8-inch rings\**
*3 to 3 1/2 lb. cut-up chicken*
*1 small lemon, thinly sliced*
*1/2 cup cognac*
*2 tablespoons olive oil*
*2 tablespoons butter*
*Salt and freshly ground pepper*

1. Heat oven to 400°F. Arrange apple slices in 13x9-inch baking dish. Top apples with chicken.
2. Arrange lemon slices over chicken. Drizzle with cognac and oil. Dot with butter. Season to taste with salt and pepper.
3. Bake, uncovered, about 1 hour or until chicken is fork-tender and juices run clear.

\*If you don't have an apple corer, quarter apple and cut into 3/8-inch slices.

4 servings

You know, these are family recipes, home cooking, what people make regularly.

# *Postre de Naranja*

## Double Orange Dessert

3 or 4 oranges, peeled
1 tablespoon orange-flavored liqueur (such as Cointreau) or orange juice
1 teaspoon sugar*
1/2 cup whipping cream, whipped**

1. Slice oranges; arrange on serving plate. Spoon orange-flavored liqueur over oranges; sprinkle with sugar.
2. Spoon whipped cream onto oranges.
*Coarsely granulated sugar looks pretty, but regular sugar tastes good, too.
**If desired, add a small amount of orange-flavored liqueur to the whipped cream.

4 servings

Deceptively simple...
a nice finish to a
heavy meal.

# Manzanas al Horno

## Baked Apples with Cognac

*Irma Galán*

"I'm a pastry chef. I've worked in the pastry shop since I finished school. Sure, I take courses, but mostly I learn on the job. The shop has been in the family for over 19 years. Our kind of pastries could be made at home, but what happens is that women don't have much practice and they don't have the time."

*4 baking apples*

*1/2 cup water*

*1 cinnamon stick*

*1 piece lemon peel*

*4 tablespoons cognac or brandy*

*4 tablespoons sugar*

1. Heat oven to 350°F. Core apples without piercing bottom; place apples in shallow baking pan. Add water, cinnamon stick and lemon peel to pan.
2. Spoon 1 tablespoon cognac into center of each apple. Sprinkle each with 1 tablespoon sugar. Cover pan with foil.
3. Bake 40 to 50 minutes or until apples are tender when pierced with toothpick. Serve warm or cold.

4 servings

Delicious served
with a pour
of cream.

# *Coquitos*

## Coconut Macaroons

3 eggs
1 1/2 cups sugar
1 (10-oz.) pkg. flaked unsweetened coconut

1. Heat oven to 300°F. Line cookie sheets with parchment paper or grease and lightly flour.
2. Beat eggs in large bowl. Add sugar; mix at high speed until mixture is thick and lemon colored. Stir in coconut. Shape mixture into 1 1/2-inch balls; place on lined cookie sheets.
3. Bake about 20 minutes or until golden. Remove from oven; let stand on cookie sheets for 2 minutes. Remove from cookie sheets; place on wire racks. Cool completely. Store in tightly-covered container.

Makes 3 dozen

The quintessential macaroon!
Crispy, chewy, sweet.

Taste!

# Torta de Limón

## Lemon Cake

| | |
|---|---|
| 2 eggs | 2 cups flour |
| 1 cup sugar | 2 teaspoons baking powder |
| 1 cup milk | 1 tablespoon sugar |
| 1/2 cup vegetable oil | 1 cup whipping cream, whipped |
| Grated peel from 1 lemon | Fruit |
|   (2 to 3 teaspoons) | |

1. Heat oven to 325°F.* Grease and flour 9- or 8-inch glass baking pan.
2. In bowl, beat eggs and 1 cup sugar until thickened. Add milk, oil and lemon peel; mix well. Add flour and baking powder; mix until well blended. Pour into pan. Sprinkle with 1 tablespoon sugar.
3. Bake 25 to 30 minutes or until top is golden brown and toothpick inserted in center comes out clean. Serve with whipped cream and your choice of fruit.

*Increase oven temperature to 350°F. if using a metal pan.

8 or 9 servings

This light, lemony cake is great topped with fruit and whipped cream or ice cream.

# Rollitos de Anís

## Anise Cookies

| | |
|---|---|
| 1/2 cup sugar | 2 1/2 cups flour |
| 3/4 cup vegetable oil | 2 teaspoons baking powder |
| 1/2 cup anise-flavored liqueur (such as sambuca) | 1/2 teaspoon salt |
| 1 egg | Sugar |

1. In large bowl, combine 1/2 cup sugar, oil, liqueur and egg; mix well. Stir in flour, baking powder and salt until well mixed. (Dough will seem soft and oily.) For easier handling, cover and refrigerate dough for at least 30 minutes.
2. Heat oven to 400°F. Cookies can be made two ways:
   a) Shape dough into 1-inch balls; place on ungreased cookie sheets. Flatten with bottom of glass dipped in sugar.
   b) Shape 1-inch balls of dough into rolls, 1 1/2 inches long, 1/2 inch wide and 1/2 inch high; place on ungreased cookie sheets. Lightly sprinkle tops with sugar.
3. Bake cookies until bottoms and edges are golden brown. Bake round cookies for 7 to 8 minutes; bake rolls for 9 to 11 minutes. Immediately remove from cookie sheets; place on wire racks. Cool completely. Store in tightly-covered container.

Makes 4 dozen

The dough is much easier to work with if well chilled.

# Arròs Sec

## Rice with Chorizo

*Rosa Prats i Novau*
*(from my mother-in-law Milagros Crespo)*

"Fixing a dish for someone you love is like giving that person a hug. Whether it's your spouse, your mother, a friend or a neighbor, you think about them and ask yourself, 'what would they like, what would surprise them?' Cooking is one of the few creative activities I like and know how to do."

| | |
|---|---|
| *1 tablespoon olive oil* | *1 small pinch saffron, crumbled* |
| *2 chorizos, sliced* | *1 3/4 cups chicken broth* |
| *1 medium tomato, peeled, chopped\** | *Tomato slices* |
| *1 garlic clove, chopped* | *Bottled spicy chiles (such as guindillas* |
| *1 cup short-grain (Arborio) rice* | *or jalapeños)* |

1. Heat oil in medium saucepan over medium heat until hot. Add chorizo slices, tomato and garlic; cook until chorizos are browned. Drain.
2. Add rice and saffron; mix well. Stir in chicken broth. Bring to a boil. Reduce heat; cover and simmer 15 minutes or until rice is almost done but still chewy and most of broth is absorbed.
3. Remove saucepan from heat. Let stand, covered, 5 to 10 minutes before serving to finish cooking. Serve with tomatoes and spicy chiles.

*See page 35.

4 servings

As my mother-in-law says, 'Daily cooking has no special charm, but I like to cook for those I love: my children, my daughter-in-law, my husband, my grandson. To prepare the dishes they like best, the way they like them best is to give them a gift, which, of course, makes me happy.'

Cocinero
COOK

# Arròs al Forn

## Oven-Baked Rice

| | |
|---|---|
| 1/2 cup dried or 1 1/4 cup canned garbanzo beans | 1 medium baking potato, cut into 1/4-inch-thick slices |
| 2 1/2 teaspoons salt | 1 cup short-grain (Arborio) rice |
| 1 tablespoon olive oil | 1 teaspoon paprika |
| 2 oz. salt pork, sliced | Pinch saffron |
| 4 whole sausages (such as Italian sweet, white Spanish butifarra or other savory sausage) | 1 tomato, cut into 8 wedges |
| | 2 cups beef broth or water |
| | 1 head garlic |

1. If using dried garbanzo beans, soak overnight in water to cover. Drain; cook in water to cover with 1 teaspoon of the salt for 45 to 60 minutes or until tender. Drain; cool.
2. Heat oven to 325°F. Heat oil in large cazuela (a wide, shallow earthenware casserole) or ovenproof skillet over low heat until hot. Add salt pork and whole sausages; cook until sausages are browned but not thoroughly cooked. Remove sausages from cazuela; drain on paper towels. Remove salt pork when browned; drain.
3. Increase heat to medium; add potato slices to cazuela; cook until browned. Add garbanzo beans, rice, paprika and saffron; sauté several minutes.
4. Stir in tomato, beef broth and remaining 1 1/2 teaspoons salt. Bring to a boil. Return sausages and salt pork; place head of garlic in center.
5. Bake 20 minutes or until rice is almost done but still chewy. Remove cazuela from oven; cover lightly with foil. Let stand 5 to 10 minutes before serving to finish cooking.

4 to 6 servings

Cooking is more than just preparing food, more than just covering a basic necessity. It's using a creative part of your brain ... watching the food be transformed.

# Andalucía

The provinces of Andalucía are Almería, Cádiz, Córdoba, Granada, Huelva, Jaén, Malaga, and Sevilla.

When the Arabs arrived in Andalucía in the 8th Century, the land was barely cultivated, and there were often shortages of essential foods. The ruling Arab class, the Omeya, encouraged agricultural growth and, by constructing dams, irrigation channels, and windmills, made it possible to farm for the first time. A culinary change took place as well when Arab spices—pepper, cinnamon, cilantro, cumin—were blended with the indigenous olive and vine. This mix, in turn, crossed the ocean to America and returned enriched by new foods, such as potatoes, corn and tomatoes. Andalusians have always had a gastronomic flair. They banished eating in the kitchen and moved into the dining room. Meals began and ended with hand washing, a custom which endured until the 18th century. The Omeya were also influential in the way food was served, in a special order instead of all at once. First, soups and broths, then, in sequence, cold hors d'oeuvres, fish in escabeche, stewed and roasted meats, and sweets. This has had a profound influence on the way food is eaten in Spain today.

*Plaza de Toros de la Real Maestranza, Sevilla*

Córdoba, in the 11th century, was considered Europe's most cultured capital. It was home to philosophers, scientists, artists and scholars; a place where Jews, Muslims and Christians lived in harmony. Even after the Moors were conquered and the culture dismantled in the 13th century, Córdoba retained its influence. Today it is a center for artists, and many bullfighting and flamenco greats. **Gazpacho**, the refreshing tomato, olive oil, garlic and pepper soup, is probably at its best in Córdoba. As is **Salmorejo**—made with the same ingredients, but thick enough to eat with a fork. Arab-inspired sweets include Pastel Cordobés, a puff pastry filled with shredded squash; honey-almond Alfajores; and tender **Polvorones** cookies.

Sevilla is a fertile land that gets about 3,000 hours of sun a year— perfect weather for sampling tapas, the miniature meals that are shared with friends (or acquaintances) at a bar or series of bars. No place has come close to the variety of tapas found in Sevilla, from a simple plate of olives or sausage to a menu's worth of delicious combinations: Huevas Fritas (fried roe with mayonnaise), Pinchos Morunos (barbecued beef

Choral book, no. 70, fol. 44; Exemo. Cabildo Metropolitano de la Catedral, Granada (opposite)

169

skewers), Pavías de Pescado (pieces of cod, floured and fried in olive oil), Caracoles (snails), Meundo (tripe). A seemingly endless array! Sevilla's famous sons and daughters include the Romans, Trajan and Hadrian; the noted lover, Don Juan; and Carmen de Prosper Merimée, heroine of the opera, Carmen.

Granada, with its gardens and flower-filled streets, is one of Spain's most visited cities. It was, for a time, the capital of Moorish Andalucía and is home to the world-famous fortress-palace, the Alhambra. The celebrated caves of Sacromonte, where gypsies lived for centuries, now offer dazzling flamenco shows. Granada's varied climate and terrain have helped create an inspired cuisine: Jamón de Trévelez—mountain ham cured in the snow; Habas a la Granadina—fava beans fried with Trévelez ham and local herbs; Migas Alpujarreñas—a hearty dish based on bread crumbs; and Moragas de Sardinas—fresh anchovies on a spit, stuck into the sand and surrounded by hot embers.

Although Pescaíto Frito, fish dipped in special batter and fried in plenty of olive oil, is fixed throughout Andalucía, the two best places to try it are Cádiz and Málaga.

In Cádiz, it is sold in fish stalls or shops, and the recipe's secret is hard to define. Is it the oil, or the mixture of fish? Málaga specializes in Boquerón, fresh baby anchovies fried in huge piles and mounded on plates. Other Málaga specialties are Ajo Blanco, an almond and garlic gazpacho served with grapes; and dark, warm muscatel wine.

Jaén has retained a quiet, simple beauty and a passion for tradition. It produces the most olive oil in the country, which shows in its culinary specialties such as Pipirrana—a mixture of green pepper, onion, tomato, and pieces of marinated fish, all seasoned with oil. From Huelva province comes Jabugo, the best ham produced in Andalucía, and in the spring, baskets full of juicy strawberries. Almería's cuisine features savory fare such as Ajo Colorao—a mix of potatoes, peppers, onions and garlic, accompanied by corn fritters.

Andalusian Jerez (sherry) is sipping wine, not from a definite crop, but from mixtures made over the years. Flavor differences are subtle among the ten official types: Fino, Amontillado, Oloroso, Palo Cortado, Raya, Pedro Ximénez, Moscatel, Sweet Wines, Color, and Manzanilla.

*The Alcázar, historic palace, Sevilla*

# Sopa de Pescado a la Abuela

## My Grandmother's Fish Soup

*Sabina Montoya Vilar*

"My grandmother was a very good cook; she had a restaurant. There were salesmen who came from another town, carrying their wares. They said to her, 'Señora Mariquita, we came here to eat paella because it's better than anyplace.' My grandmother was famous for her rice dishes."

### Soup

1 lb. firm white fish (such as cod,
    snapper or halibut)
6 cups water
1/4 cup cubed prosciutto or serrano ham
2 garlic cloves, chopped
6 whole peppercorns, crushed
2 sprigs fresh parsley

### Sofrito

2 tablespoons olive oil
1 medium onion
1 medium tomato, halved, grated
1 teaspoon salt
1/4 teaspoon pepper
1 bay leaf

2 tablespoons fresh lemon juice
2 egg yolks
1/4 teaspoon crumbled saffron

1. Cut fish into bite-sized pieces; place in large saucepan. Add all remaining soup ingredients. Bring to a boil. Reduce heat; cover and simmer 15 minutes.
2. Meanwhile, prepare sofrito. Heat olive oil in large skillet over medium heat until hot. Add rest of ingredients; cook until softened, stirring frequently.
3. Add sofrito to soup. Just before serving, stir in lemon juice, egg yolks and saffron; cook and stir over medium heat until broth is thickened slightly.

6 servings

This recipe is from Andalucía, from my grandmother. What I make is the cooking from my town.

# Espárragos con Salsa

## Asparagus with Savory Sauce

| | |
|---|---|
| 4 to 5 tablespoons olive oil | 1/2 teaspoon paprika |
| 1/2 medium onion, chopped | 1 (3/8-inch-thick) slice French bread |
| 2 garlic cloves, peeled | 2 tablespoons white wine vinegar |
| 1/2 teaspoon salt | 2 lb. asparagus spears |

1. Heat 3 tablespoons of the oil in large skillet over medium heat until hot. Add onion; sauté until it just begins to brown.
2. With slotted spoon, remove onion from skillet; place in food processor or mortar, leaving oil in skillet. Add garlic, salt and paprika to onion; process until slightly chunky.
3. In same skillet, fry bread until golden. Add fried bread and vinegar to mixture in food processor; process until mixture is still slightly chunky.
4. In large skillet, place remaining 1 to 2 tablespoons oil. Add some of asparagus in single layer. Cook over medium heat 5 to 10 minutes or until tender, turning occasionally. Repeat with remaining asparagus.
5. Arrange asparagus on serving platter. Top with onion mixture.

8 servings

Excellent. Sauce can be used to complement other dishes.

# Sepia a la Plancha

## Grilled Cuttlefish (or Squid)

*1 lb. cuttlefish or squid\**
*1 cup chopped fresh parsley*
*1/2 cup olive oil*
*3 garlic cloves, chopped*
*1 teaspoon salt*
*1/4 teaspoon pepper*

1. Rinse cuttlefish; pat dry. (If using squid and it is large, slit open along one side to make a single layer.)
2. In food processor or blender, combine all remaining ingredients; process until smooth. Reserve 1/2 cup for sauce.
3. Coat cuttlefish with remaining mixture. Let stand at room temperature 30 minutes to marinate.
4. Heat grill. Drain cuttlefish; discard marinade. Arrange on grill over hot coals; cook about 2 minutes on each side. Season to taste with additional salt and pepper. Cut cuttlefish into pieces; serve with reserved sauce.

*See page 27.

8 appetizer servings

My cooking is very simple ... everything grilled, 'a la plancha.'

COOK

# Tortilla de Ajo Tierno

## Spring Garlic Omelet

3 tablespoons olive oil
1 medium onion, chopped
2 cups sliced (1/2-inch) spring garlic or garlic scapes*
5 to 6 eggs
Salt and freshly ground pepper

1. Heat 2 tablespoons of the oil in large nonstick skillet over medium heat until hot. Add onion; sauté until softened. Add spring garlic; sauté about 5 minutes, stirring occasionally. With slotted spoon, remove onion and spring garlic from skillet; drain on paper towel. Reserve 1 tablespoon oil in skillet.
2. In medium bowl, lightly beat eggs with salt and pepper. Stir in onion and spring garlic.
3. Heat reserved 1 tablespoon oil in skillet over high heat until hot. Pour egg mixture into skillet; move skillet back and forth over burner to cook evenly. Reduce heat to medium-high; cook about 3 minutes or until bottom is browned, loosening edges with spoon if mixture sticks to sides of skillet.
4. Cover skillet with plate or large lid; invert skillet so omelet flips onto plate. Slide omelet back into skillet to cook other side. Repeat until both sides are golden and omelet is still juicy inside.
5. Cut omelet into wedges. Serve warm or at room temperature.

*Spring garlic or garlic scapes are available in the spring at farmers' markets, co-ops and some supermarkets.

4 to 6 servings

A make-ahead idea for breakfast
or brunch.

# *Natillas*

## Creamy Custard

4 cups whole milk
1 cinnamon stick
Peel from 1 lemon
1 cup sugar
4 teaspoons cornstarch
8 egg yolks
Cinnamon

1. In medium saucepan, bring milk, cinnamon stick and lemon peel to a boil over medium heat. Reduce heat; simmer 2 minutes. Remove from heat. Remove cinnamon stick and lemon peel.
2. In top of double boiler or in heavy saucepan, combine sugar and cornstarch; mix well. Add egg yolks. If using double boiler, heat over boiling water; if using saucepan, heat over low heat. Cook, beating mixture with wire whisk or wooden spoon until sugar is dissolved and mixture turns pale yellow.
3. Slowly add milk mixture to egg yolk mixture, cooking and stirring constantly until mixture comes to a boil and thickens. Remove from heat. Place double boiler or saucepan in pan of cold water; stir to cool mixture. Pour into individual dessert dishes or large flat dish. Refrigerate until serving time.
4. Just before serving, sprinkle with cinnamon. Serve with biscotti or wafer cookies.

6 to 8 servings

I especially liked the light texture compared to other custard desserts I have had.

# Gazpacho Manchego

## Chicken Gazpacho from La Mancha

*Ceferina Montoya (with Sabina Montoya Vilar)*

"I've lived in Barcelona about 30 years. I'm from a little town in Granada. ...In the old days women made the dough which is cooked in this soup, but it takes a lot of time. So, now it's sold already made."

| | |
|---|---|
| 3 tablespoons olive oil | 3 branches spring garlic, sliced* |
| 1 to 1 1/2 lb. boneless, skinless chicken thighs | 4 cups water |
| Salt and freshly ground pepper | 1 1/2 teaspoons salt |
| 1 medium red onion, chopped | 1/4 teaspoon pepper |
| 1 medium red bell pepper, chopped | 1 bay leaf |
| 1 medium green bell pepper, chopped | Few threads of saffron, crumbled |
| 1 medium tomato, coarsely chopped | 1 to 1 1/2 cups wide egg noodles** |
| 2 garlic cloves, chopped | 1 cup frozen lima beans |

1. Heat oil in saucepot or Dutch oven over medium-high heat until hot. Add chicken thighs; cover and cook on all sides until browned. Season to taste with salt and pepper. Remove chicken; set aside.
2. In same saucepot, reduce heat to medium; add onion, red and green bell pepper, tomato, garlic and spring garlic; sauté 10 to 15 minutes or until softened.
3. Stir in browned chicken, water, 1 1/2 teaspoons salt, 1/4 teaspoon pepper, bay leaf and saffron. Bring to a boil. Reduce heat; cover and simmer about 15 minutes or until chicken is tender.
4. Add noodles and lima beans. Return to a boil. Simmer, uncovered, about 10 minutes or until noodles are done. Remove bay leaf before serving.

*Spring garlic is available in the spring at farmers' markets, co-ops and some supermarkets.

**Bow tie pasta can also be used.

4 to 6 servings

Excellent. A 3-star dish!

Taster

# Espinaca Cortada

## Almond-Crusted Spinach Balls

| | |
|---|---|
| 1 egg, beaten | 1/4 teaspoon salt |
| 1 (10-oz.) pkg. frozen chopped spinach, thawed, liquid squeezed out | 1/4 teaspoon freshly ground pepper |
| 1/2 cup bread crumbs | 1/2 cup almonds, finely chopped |
| 1/4 cup chopped fresh parsley | Olive oil for frying |

1. In medium bowl, combine egg, spinach, bread crumbs, parsley, salt and pepper; mix well. Shape into 20 to 24 (1-inch) balls. Coat with chopped almonds.
2. Heat 3/4 inch of oil in medium skillet over high heat until very hot. Add half of spinach balls; fry until golden brown. Drain on paper towels. Repeat with remaining half of balls. Serve warm.

20 to 24 tapas

Great with wine.

# Pierna de Cordero

## Leg of Lamb with Ham and Parsley

| | |
|---|---|
| 3 oz. prosciutto or serrano ham, thinly sliced (1/2 cup) | 1 (3 to 4-lb.) leg of lamb |
| 1/2 cup chopped fresh parsley | 1 tablespoon olive oil |
| 1/2 teaspoon salt | Freshly ground pepper |
| | 1/2 cup dry white wine |

1. Heat oven to 450°F. In food processor or with mortar and pestle, process ham, parsley and salt until paste consistency.
2. Place lamb in roasting pan. Score top about 3/4 inch deep. Stuff with ham mixture. Pour oil over top; season to taste with pepper.
3. Roast at 450°F. for 15 minutes. Reduce oven temperature to 350°F.; roast about 45 to 60 minutes or until lamb reaches desired doneness. (Roast 12 to 20 minutes per pound, depending on desired doneness. Meat thermometer should reach 140°F. for rare, 155°F. for medium.)
4. About 5 minutes before lamb is done, pour wine over lamb.*

*The lamb is traditionally served with sliced pears and apples, and boiled potatoes.

8 servings

Bravo! The stuffing enhanced the
lovely flavor of the lamb.

# *Polvorones*

## Almond Shortbreads

| | |
|---|---|
| 2 cups flour | 1/4 teaspoon salt |
| 1 cup butter, softened | 1/4 teaspoon cinnamon |
| 4 oz. (3/4 cup) blanched almonds, finely chopped | 2 teaspoons grated lemon peel (about 1/2 lemon) |
| 1/2 cup sugar | Powdered sugar, if desired |

1. Heat oven to 325°F. Spread 1 cup of the flour on large cookie sheet. Toast in oven for 8 to 10 minutes or until slightly golden, stirring occasionally. Cool. (Toasting gives cookies an additional nutty flavor.)
2. In large bowl, beat butter and almonds until fluffy. Add sugar, salt, cinnamon and lemon peel; mix well. Stir in toasted and untoasted flour until well mixed. For easier handling, cover and refrigerate dough for 30 minutes.
3. On lightly-floured surface, pat dough to about 3/8-inch thickness. With 1 1/2-inch round cutter, cut into rounds; place on ungreased cookie sheets.
4. Bake 16 to 20 minutes or until lightly browned and firm to the touch. Immediately remove from cookie sheets; place on wire racks. Cool completely. Sprinkle with powdered sugar. Store in tightly-covered container.

Makes 3 1/2 dozen

Crispy and yummy.

La Mezquita, Córdoba. 8-10 c.

España
POR AVION

The Alhambra, Granada

Contrary to popular notions, not everyone in Andalucía is out in the streets going from one tapas bar to another. But Sevilla is fun to explore on foot, and the famous places are definitely worth the visit: the Cathedral, one of the three biggest in Europe; the Alcázar, a fascinating palace of great beauty; and the old Jewish Quarter, now full of shops and restaurants. One day I took a side trip from Sevilla to Córdoba where there is another architectural masterpiece—La Mezquita, a mosque into which a cathedral was later incorporated. It's a trompe l'oeil of seemingly endless red and white painted arches. Córdoba is also home to Spain's oldest remaining synagogue.

# Carne Mechada

## Garlic-Crusted Pork Loin

*María Rosario Parrilla Navarro (Chari)*

"I work in Ana's home as a family employee and cook. ... I have a lot of cookbooks. And I experiment. If someone gives me a recipe, I say to myself, 'why cook it this way?' If I want to put in more ingredients, I do it. ... If I take a recipe from a book, I measure. But the second time, if I haven't liked the taste or the texture or something, I put in more of one thing, I put in more of another. Recipes are like that."

*Ana Martínez Jiménez*

"I have forgotten a lot of what I did automatically, that's for sure. I have a book of recipes with things from my mother, from everybody – what I've asked for. When I have to cook, I go back to the book and remember, 'you, how were you? what were you made with?' Cooking is like riding a bicycle. You lose your reflexes, but I believe when one has the touch you have it forever."

| | |
|---|---|
| 1 small head garlic, cloves separated, peeled* | 1 (3 1/2-lb.) pork loin |
| 2 teaspoons salt | 1 1/2 cups water |
| 1 teaspoon whole peppercorns | 1 cup dry white wine |
| 1 teaspoon paprika | 1/2 teaspoon dried thyme |
| 1 chicken bouillon cube | 4 whole cloves |
| 2 medium onions, sliced | Dash nutmeg |
| | 1/2 cup olive oil or 1/2 stick lard |

1. In food processor or with mortar and pestle, process garlic, salt, peppercorns, paprika and bouillon cube to make a mash to cover pork loin.
2. Layer bottom of large saucepot or Dutch oven with sliced onions. Top with pork. Pat garlic mixture over top of pork. Add water, wine, thyme, cloves and nutmeg to pan. Bring to a boil. Reduce heat; simmer, uncovered, 10 minutes.
3. Add oil; cover and simmer over low heat for 1 hour, stirring occasionally. Pork is done when internal temperature reaches 160°F. and pork is no longer pink in center. Serve pork warm or cold with sauce from pan.

*To peel garlic easily, lightly press clove with side of chef's knife. Peel should slip off.

8 servings

Chari: Carne Mechada is from my aunt. I called her and she said, 'look, you put in such and such a quantity.' I wrote it down, and I put that much in. But I don't like cloves, so I put in one. ... Carne Mechada is usually eaten as 'fiambre' (cold meat), but it's perfectly good warm too. It can also be made with veal."

# Atún Encebollado

## Tuna with Caramelized Onions

| | |
|---|---|
| 2 tablespoons olive oil | 1 bay leaf |
| 3 to 4 medium onions, thinly sliced | 1/4 teaspoon saffron |
| 2 garlic cloves, sliced | 1 cup dry white wine |
| 6 peppercorns | 1 (3/4-lb.) tuna steak* |
| 1 chicken or fish bouillon cube | |

1. Heat oil in large heavy skillet over medium heat until hot. Add onions; reduce heat; cook about 15 minutes or until onions are golden brown and reduced, stirring occasionally.
2. Add all remaining ingredients except tuna. Bring to a boil. Reduce heat; simmer 15 minutes, stirring occasionally.
3. Push onion mixture to sides of skillet. If necessary, add a little more oil. Increase heat to high; add tuna steak; sear until browned on each side. Cook to desired doneness. Cut tuna diagonally into slices. Serve with onions.

*Use sushi-grade tuna if preparing tuna rare.

6 servings

Sear the tuna, or cook to taste. Cooking a bit longer would be more traditional.

# *Rustidera*

## Baked Squid and Vegetables

| | |
|---|---|
| *4 tablespoons olive oil* | *2 medium tomatoes, sliced* |
| *1 medium onion, sliced* | *2 garlic cloves, sliced* |
| *4 medium baking potatoes, peeled, sliced* | *1 to 2 tablespoons chopped fresh parsley* |
| *1 1/2 teaspoons salt* | *1 tablespoon pine nuts* |
| *1 lb. squid, sliced* | |

1. Heat oven to 350°F. Cover bottom of heavy casserole with 1 tablespoon of the oil. Layer onion and potato slices in casserole. Sprinkle with 1 teaspoon of the salt; drizzle with 1 tablespoon of the remaining oil.
2. Add squid; sprinkle with remaining 1/2 teaspoon salt; drizzle with another tablespoon of the oil.
3. Top with tomato slices, garlic, parsley and pine nuts. Drizzle with the remaining tablespoon oil.
4. Bake, uncovered, 45 minutes or until squid and potatoes are tender.

4 servings

Ana: Here we only use olive oil. We use it pure, and for everything. ... In addition, we're from Jaén, the province where the most oil is produced.

# Manzanas en la Microonda

## Orange-Spiced Apples in the Microwave

3 baking apples
3/4 cup water
2 cinnamon sticks
Grated peel from 1 orange (1 to 1 1/2 tablespoons)

1. Cut each apple into 8 sections. Core; cut into 1/2-inch-thick pieces. Place in microwave-safe baking dish.
2. Mix water, cinnamon sticks and orange peel; pour over apples.
3. Microwave on High for 7 to 8 minutes or until apples are tender, stirring once halfway through cooking. Serve warm or cold.*

*If desired, serve with sweetened whipped cream.

4 servings

Chari: When Ana's mother came and lived here for a month I didn't cook. I didn't go in the kitchen at all. When she left, I went back, to begin to make what I had forgotten.

# *Huevos a la Flamenca*

## Eggs Flamenco

*Rosario González García*

"When I got married at 16, I knew how to do all the jobs in the house except cooking. So I got up the first day and grabbed 5 pesetas and called my mother. I said, 'Mama, today I'm going to make lentils. What do I buy?' Every day I took the shopping basket, and the 5 pesetas to call her. And as days passed, and months and years, I had bags and bags of all the recipes. All of them. The first one I put in was the lentils. I'd like to do a cookbook, really, because I have it all saved. I have, let's say, infinite recipes."

| | |
|---|---|
| *1 tablespoon olive oil* | *2 garlic cloves, chopped* |
| *3 medium tomatoes, seeded, chopped* | *4 eggs* |
| *1 medium green bell pepper, chopped* | *Salt and freshly ground pepper* |
| *1/2 medium onion, chopped* | *2 tablespoons chopped fresh parsley* |

1. Heat oil in large skillet over medium heat until hot. Add tomatoes, bell pepper, onion and garlic; sauté until softened and liquid evaporates.
2. Move vegetables to form 4 round sections for eggs. Break 1 egg into each section. Season to taste with salt and pepper. Cover; cook 5 to 8 minutes or until eggs are done.
3. Carefully spoon eggs and vegetables onto individual plates. Sprinkle with parsley.

4 servings

Delicious and colorful for brunch or a light supper.

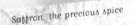

*Saffron, the precious spice*

Spring, 2000. I arrived in Barcelona just in
time for an international food show. Wandering
around for hours, I tasted far more bread
cubes with olive oil than I had intended,
while looking for contacts and companies that
were exporting Spanish products to the United
States. My most fortuitous discovery, however,
was at the booth of Azfrán Natural, a saffron
company, where they told me about the winner
of a recipe contest they had staged. Chosen in
a drawing among 50 finalists, she was the one
everyone had been rooting for. Married at 16,
she had never been able to go on a honeymoon.
Her prize—a long "honeymoon" weekend in
Paris. It was such a sweet story I asked if I
could talk to her and, if she agreed, put her
in the book. As it turned out she was more
than happy to meet me, to give me the winning
recipe, Popurrí de Pescado, and many more.

# *Popurrí de Pescado*

## Potpourri of Fish with Saffron

1 1/2 lb. mixed firm white fish
  (such as monkfish, halibut or snapper)
3 cups water
1 onion, quartered
1 medium red bell pepper, quartered
1 teaspoon salt
4 peppercorns
2 tablespoons olive oil
1 medium onion, chopped

1 garlic clove, chopped
1 medium tomato, peeled, chopped*
1 cup fine noodles

### Mash
2 tablespoons chopped fresh parsley
1 garlic clove, chopped
1/4 teaspoon saffron, crumbled
Salt and freshly ground pepper

1. Rinse fish; pat dry. Place in bottom of large saucepan or Dutch oven. Add water, quartered onion, bell pepper, 1 teaspoon salt and peppercorns. Bring to a boil, skimming off any scum and froth from surface.
2. Reduce heat; simmer, uncovered, about 15 minutes or until fish flakes easily with fork, skimming surface often.
3. Remove fish from saucepan. Strain broth.
4. Add oil to same saucepan; heat over medium heat until hot. Add chopped onion and 1 chopped garlic clove; sauté until softened. Add tomato; simmer slowly until soft.
5. Cut fish into bite-sized pieces; add to saucepan with strained broth and noodles. Bring to a boil. Reduce heat; simmer about 5 minutes or until noodles are cooked.
6. Meanwhile, in food processor or with mortar and pestle, process parsley, 1 chopped garlic clove and saffron. Add mash to soup during last few minutes of cooking time. Season to taste with salt and pepper.

*See page 35.

6 servings

It's an original recipe. Winning the contest gave me the satisfaction of knowing I could cook. What happens is that at home they don't value the work of cooking. They come every day and eat and, nothing. But I won a fantastic trip, a dream trip. I have never traveled, never, never. But I love to know new things, new cities, new cultures, all that. It feeds me, it satisfies me.

# Chocos con Patatas

## Cuttlefish (or Squid) with Potatoes

2 tablespoons olive oil

1 medium onion, chopped

2 garlic cloves, chopped

1 medium red bell pepper, chopped

1 medium tomato, chopped

2 bay leaves

1 lb. cuttlefish or squid, sliced*

1/2 cup dry white wine

2 medium to large baking potatoes, sliced

Water

### Mash

1 garlic clove, chopped

2 tablespoons chopped fresh parsley

1 teaspoon salt

1/2 teaspoon cumin

1/2 teaspoon saffron

1. Heat oil in large saucepan over medium heat until hot. Add onion; sauté until softened. Add garlic, bell pepper, tomato and bay leaves; sauté until softened.
2. Rinse cuttlefish; pat dry; add to saucepan. Add wine; bring to a boil. Simmer, uncovered, about 10 minutes to reduce wine. Cover; simmer an additional 15 minutes.
3. Stir in potato slices; barely cover with water. Bring to a boil. Reduce heat; cover and simmer 15 minutes or until cuttlefish and potatoes are tender.
4. Meanwhile, in food processor or with mortar and pestle, process all mash ingredients. If desired, add a little wine for easier processing.
5. Stir mash into cuttlefish and potatoes. Serve in individual bowls with crusty French bread.

*See page 27.

4 servings

The tender squid was tasty and seemed to feel good against the grainy texture of the potatoes.

Taster

# Almejas con Fideos Gordos

## Clams with Thick Noodles

| | |
|---|---|
| 1 1/2 lb. clams | 4 garlic cloves, chopped |
| 1/2 lb. shrimp, shelled, deveined | 6 cups liquid (broth from cooked clams, |
| 3 cups water | plus purchased clam broth and water) |
| 2 tablespoons olive oil | 1 cup wide egg noodles or bow tie pasta |
| 1 medium onion, chopped | 1 chicken or fish bouillon cube |
| 1 medium green bell pepper, | 2 bay leaves |
| coarsely chopped | 2 tablespoons chopped fresh parsley |
| 1 medium tomato, coarsely chopped | |

1. Scrub clams under cold running water. Rinse shrimp; set aside.
2. Bring 3 cups water to a boil in large saucepan. Add clams; cook, uncovered, until clams open. Remove clams from saucepan as they open to prevent toughening. Strain broth into another container; reserve.
3. Heat oil in same large saucepan over medium heat until hot. Add onion; sauté until softened. Add bell pepper, tomato and garlic; sauté several minutes or until softened.
4. Measure cooking liquid from clams, purchased clam broth and water to total 6 cups; add to saucepan. Bring to a boil. Add egg noodles, bouillon cube and bay leaves. Reduce heat; simmer until noodles are tender, adding clams, shrimp and parsley during last 5 minutes of cooking time. Remove bay leaves before serving.

4 servings

Possibly the best soup I've ever had. The mixture of textures was appealing to the eye and wonderful to the palate.

# Estofado de Ternera

## Spicy Veal Stew

### Sofrito
2 tablespoons olive oil

1 medium onion, chopped

1 medium tomato, halved, grated

1 medium green bell pepper, chopped

3 garlic cloves, chopped

2 bay leaves

### Veal and Potatoes
1 1/2 lb. boneless veal, cut into
  1 1/2-inch pieces

Salt and freshly ground pepper

1 cup dry white wine

1 cup water

6 medium red potatoes, peeled, cut into
  bite-sized pieces

### Mash
1 to 2 spicy chiles (such as jalapeños),
  seeded, chopped

2 garlic cloves, chopped

1 chicken bouillon cube

1 tablespoon chopped fresh parsley

1/2 teaspoon salt

1/2 teaspoon cumin

1. Heat oil in large saucepan or Dutch oven over medium heat until hot. Add all remaining sofrito ingredients; cook until softened.
2. Increase heat to medium-high; add veal; cook until browned, stirring constantly. Season to taste with salt and pepper. Add wine and water. Reduce heat; cover and simmer 25 minutes.
3. Meanwhile, in food processor or with mortar and pestle, process all mash ingredients.
4. Add potatoes and mash to stew. Simmer 25 to 30 minutes or until veal is tender and potatoes are softened. Remove bay leaves before serving.

4 to 6 servings

Here in Sevilla, we still give some time to the siesta, but there are fewer people who do because the labor market doesn't give you the option. Everything is changing. I think there should be time at meals to dedicate to your family. Every day we're together less, and I miss it.

# Espinacas con Garbanzos

## Cumin-Scented Spinach with Garbanzos  *Eva María Lopez-Cepero Mora*

"I love to cook, I love to eat ... more than anything, Mediterranean food and the foods of the season. I identify with the Mediterranean culture; it's part of my own culture. My mother passed this on to me. ... I think we've lost a lot of our traditional cooking and it has a value that we have to recover. If we don't pay attention we're going to lose it."

| | |
|---|---|
| 3 tablespoons olive oil | 2 tablespoons water |
| 6 garlic cloves, peeled | 2 lb. fresh spinach, cooked, drained |
| 2 teaspoons salt | 1 cup dried or 2 1/2 cups canned |
| 2 teaspoons cumin | garbanzo beans |
| 1 (3/4-inch-thick) slice baguette | 2 teaspoons paprika |
| 2 tablespoons white wine vinegar | |

1. If using dried garbanzo beans, soak beans overnight in water to cover. Drain, cook in water to cover with 1 teaspoon of the salt for 45 to 60 minutes or until tender. Drain; cool.
2. Heat oil in medium skillet over medium heat until hot. Add garlic; sauté until it just begins to brown. Using food processor or mortar and pestle, process garlic, remaining teaspoon salt and cumin.
3. In remaining oil in skillet, fry baguette slice until golden. Place in small bowl; pour vinegar and water over bread. Let soak for several minutes. Add to garlic mixture in food processor; process.
4. In Dutch oven or cazuela (a wide, shallow earthenware casserole), combine spinach, garbanzo beans, garlic mixture, oil remaining in skillet and paprika; cook until thoroughly heated.

6 servings

I'm not accustomed to eating spicy food like I ate in the U.S. Here the food isn't very spicy.

Palacio de Carlos V, the Alhambra, Granada

*View from the Alhambra*

The Spanish government offers a series of booklets for the main cities with various walking itineraries. The problem, other than my directional disability, is that not all the streets are named on the tiny maps. So, on my walks I invariably lost a few churches and convents, and who-knows-what portal or decorative trim. But, in the end, what difference did it make? I eventually managed to stumble upon them. In Granada, however, even I couldn't miss the Alhambra. Its palaces, fortress and gardens are high on a hill overlooking the city and beyond. From within, the Moorish designs are incredibly beautiful—once-painted filigreed arches, decorated wooden ceilings, graceful lines. And from elsewhere, the Sierra Nevada gives the Alhambra a dramatic backdrop.

On the bus back to Sevilla, the woman behind me was wearing so much perfume I asked the driver if I could sit by him in the jump seat. Though he was reluctant, he let me. What a fine view I had! Olive groves, fields of wheat, tree farms— a lovely green and brown quilt covering the land.

# Roscos de Naranja

## Orange Ring Cookies

*Basilisa Espin*

"I never went any place to learn to cook. I learned at home from my mother and then from friends. I was a girl! ... When my son did his baccalaureate, I had five students staying in the house and with what they paid me, my son was able to study. I had to be cooking every day. I don't make little bits of food, not at all. I have to make a lot. Always. Always."

| | |
|---|---|
| 3 eggs | 4 cups flour |
| 1 cup sugar | 1/2 teaspoon baking soda |
| 1/2 cup vegetable oil | 1/2 teaspoon salt |
| Grated peel from 4 oranges | Sugar |
| 1/4 cup orange juice | |

1. Heat oven to 350°F. Grease cookie sheets. In large bowl, beat eggs and 1 cup sugar until thickened. Add oil, orange peel and orange juice; mix well.
2. Stir in flour, baking soda and salt until well mixed. For easier handling, cover and refrigerate dough for at least 30 minutes.
3. On lightly floured surface, roll pieces of dough into long ropes, about 1/2 inch thick. Cut into 4-inch pieces; shape each into circle. Dip in sugar; place on greased cookie sheets.
4. Bake 20 to 25 minutes or until tops are light golden brown. Immediately remove from cookie sheets; place on wire racks. Cool completely. Store in tightly-covered container.

Makes 4 dozen

I always did cake, homemade sweets, pastry. Mine turned out extremely well. We didn't buy; what's made at home is better. At Easter we had Roscos and they were delicious. My husband enjoyed eating sweets, and I always made them for him.

# *Paella Mixta*

## Chicken and Seafood Paella

| | |
|---|---|
| 4 tablespoons olive oil | 1/2 lb. fresh green beans |
| 1 lb. boneless, skinless chicken thighs, halved | 1 medium tomato, halved, grated |
| 1/2 lb. shrimp, shelled with tails left on | 2 teaspoons salt |
| 1/2 lb. squid, sliced into rings | 1 teaspoon saffron |
| 1 medium onion, chopped | 1/2 teaspoon freshly ground pepper |
| 1 medium red bell pepper, chopped | 9 cups chicken broth* |
| 4 garlic cloves, chopped | 1 lb. clams, well-rinsed |
| 3 cups short-grain (Arborio) rice | 1 lemon, cut into thin wedges |
| 2 medium artichokes, trimmed, quartered and choke removed | 2 tablespoons toasted pine nuts, if desired |

1. Heat 2 tablespoons oil in paella pan or large skillet over medium-high heat until hot. Add chicken thighs; brown about 2 minutes on each side. Remove from pan.
2. Add shrimp; sauté about 2 minutes or until pink. Remove from pan. Add squid; cook and toss about 2 minutes or until opaque. Remove from pan. Wipe pan with paper towels.
3. Reduce heat to medium; add remaining 2 tablespoons oil to pan. Add onion; sauté until softened. Add bell pepper and garlic; sauté until softened.
4. Add rice; sauté 1 minute, stirring constantly. Return chicken thighs and squid to pan. Stir in artichokes, green beans, tomato, salt, saffron, pepper and chicken broth. Bring to a boil. Reduce heat; simmer 15 minutes.
5. Add clams and shrimp; simmer 5 minutes or until clams open and rice is almost done but still chewy. Remove pan from heat. Cover with dish towel; let stand 5 to 10 minutes before serving to finish cooking. Garnish with lemon and pine nuts.

*If chicken broth is heated separately, the mixture will boil much faster.

8 to 12 servings

The students that stayed here would say, 'Basi, make that good paella.' They liked it a lot. One day they asked for meatballs and another day, paella. Whatever they liked I made.

## Olive Oil

There are basically three grades of olive oil:

*Extra Virgin Olive Oil* has a maximum acidity level of 0.5°, with the color, fruity flavor and aroma of fresh olives. It can range from an intense yellow to green. It is used for salads, grilled fish, vegetables, pasta, and toasted bread.

*Virgin Olive Oil* has an acidity level of less than 1.5° and is of high quality, but not as high as extra virgin. It has a fresh, fruity flavor and is used for salads, fish dishes, stews, and for frying.

*Olive Oil* is a blend of virgin olive oil and refined olive oil which gives it its color, flavor and aroma. It is used for frying and sautéing.

In addition, there is Green Oil which is made from olives picked from the tree, never from the ground, and Cold Press Oil which is made from olives crushed within two hours of picking. Cold Press Oil has an intense, fruity aroma.

*Spanish pimentón*

## Paprika

The pimiento was brought to Spain from South America in 1493 and it found a perfect climate in which to thrive. To make paprika, the pimientos are harvested and roasted over a wood fire (oak and evergreen oak) to create the characteristic color, smoky flavor and aroma. The peppers are peeled, but not washed. Spanish paprika (pimentón) became a commercial product only in the 19th century. It is available in both sweet and spicy varieties so cooks can season to taste.

### Saffron

Saffron comes from the pistils of the purple crocus flower, sativus linnaeus. To get only 1 kilo of saffron, 170,000 flowers have to be gathered by hand, and the stigmas removed from inside the petals. When dried, this becomes saffron, which has no substitute for color and aroma. Spanish saffron is considered to be the finest in the world.

Olive oils, spices, an excellent variety of vinegars and many other Spanish foods can be ordered by phone or on the Internet. See Shopping for Ingredients, page 244.

# Islas Canarias

The archipelago of the Canary Islands includes Gran Canaria, Fuerteventura, Lanzarote, Tenerife, La Palma, La Gomera, El Hierro, and a number of small rocky islands of volcanic origin. Each is very different from the rest. The island of Tenerife has so many microclimates that around every bend is another spectacular vista, with El Teide, the highest peak in Spain, overlooking it all. Walking around El Teide, which is a volcano, is like stepping onto the moon; its color range resembles a painting. The weather is wonderful, too—sunny, breezy, a springtime paradise year round. The Canary Islands were first inhabited by the Guanches, a tall, light-skinned race who lived in grottoes or circular houses. In 1496, despite a valiant fight, the Guanches were conquered by the troops of the Catholic monarchs, Ferdinand and Isabella.

The many fruits and vegetables that are cultivated in these temperate islands and the abundance of fish make Canarian cuisine at once delicious, simple and light. Though perhaps best known for its tomatoes, potatoes, bananas and other tropical fruits, Canarian cuisine has a more plentiful base. It is a cosmopolitan blend, inspired by recipes from the Peninsula (especially Castilla, Extremadura, and Andalucía), Latin America, Africa, and from its native Guanches. In the Canaries, for example, a hearty Cocido from the Peninsula is transformed into **Puchero Canario**, made with yams, squash, pears, sweet potatoes and garbanzos. It is often served with a spicy Mojo sauce.

Gofio, typically and exclusively Canarian, and once its staple food, stands as an example of Guanche cooking. Made from toasted wheat, corn, barley or garbanzo flour, gofio is used in a variety of ways. Mixed with water or milk, then shaped and sliced, it is served as a type of bread and eaten with honey. Heaped into other dishes it adds flavor and substance. Gofio is also used to make tasty desserts.

Perhaps the most "exported" Canarian recipe is Mojo, a sauce made of oil, vinegar, garlic, salt and various spices. Mojo can accompany meat, fish, potatoes, whatever you choose, and there are as many variations as there are cooks. Mixed with paprika, it becomes **Mojo Colorado**; with peppers, **Mojo Picón**; with parsley, **Mojo Verde**.

Other Canarian specialties are **Papas Arrugadas**, wrinkled potatoes cooked in very salty water; Potaje de Berros, a vegetable stew made with watercress; and Potaje de Jaramago, a stew made with a plant much like turnip greens. Meat and fish dishes include **Conejo en Salmorejo**, savory marinated rabbit; **Carne de Cabra Arreglada**, goat stew; and Cazuela de Mero, a sea bass casserole. Many renowned cheeses also come from the islands.

Desserts might include fresh fruit from the Canarian cornucopia—bananas, avocados, mangos, custard apples, papayas. Or a traditional Leche Asada, baked custard; or **Frangollo,** a cornmeal pudding made with almonds and raisins.

Canarian wines have a long history—praised even by Shakespeare—and in the 16th and 17th centuries were the principal economic engine of the islands. When the Canary Islands became the main passage between Europe and America (Columbus stopped there before leaving for the New World), its wines were exported from the Garachico harbor in Tenerife.

In Tenerife, Ycoden Daute Isora vines are grown on ash and volcanic soil in small fields and are tended using no mechanical machinery. Because there have never been phylloxera (plant lice) in Tenerife, farmers can plant in open fields. Other Denominación de Origen wines are: Tacoronte from Tenerife (particularly Listán and Negramoll), and Malvasía from Lanzarote.

As for spirits, Canarian rum is excellent. Local beverages also include Mistela—a strong coffee, sugar and eau de vie drink.

*Late afternoon. Los Silos. Tenerife (opposite)*

# Potaje de Coles

## Hearty Cabbage Stew

*Evelia Acevedo Torres*

"The hunters went out for rabbits every Thursday and Sunday and the women went to gather herbs. We women also worked in raising animals, to fatten them."

| | |
|---|---|
| 1/2 lb. dried garbanzo beans | 1/2 lb. winter squash, peeled, cut into |
| 6 cups water | bite-sized pieces* |
| 1 lb. pork ribs | 1 small onion, chopped |
| 1 teaspoon salt | 1 medium tomato, peeled, seeded |
| 1/2 medium head green cabbage, | and chopped** |
| coarsely chopped (about 5 cups) | 1 garlic clove, chopped |
| 3 to 4 medium red potatoes, peeled, cut | 1 chicken bouillon cube |
| into bite-sized pieces | 1/4 teaspoon crushed saffron |

1. Soak beans overnight in water to cover. Drain just before using.
2. Bring 6 cups water to a boil in large soup pot or Dutch oven. Add drained beans, pork ribs and salt. Return to a boil. Reduce heat; cover and simmer 45 minutes. Skim top, if necessary.
3. Add all remaining ingredients. Return to a boil. Reduce heat; cover and simmer an additional 45 minutes or until vegetables are tender and stew is of desired consistency.

*To make squash easier to peel, heat in microwave for several minutes. Cool slightly; peel.

**See page 35.

8 servings

*Market, Santiago de Compostela*

This is made either with a head of cabbage or with the open, leafy variety. Lettuce can also be added. Potaje is one of the things most typical of the Canary Islands.

# Carne Arreglada

## Slow-Cooked Beef Stew

| | |
|---|---|
| 2 tablespoons olive oil | Juice of 1 lemon |
| 2 lb. beef chuck, cut into 1 1/2-inch pieces | 1 chicken bouillon cube |
| Salt and freshly ground pepper | 2 tablespoons finely chopped fresh parsley |
| 2 medium onions, chopped | 1 tablespoon chopped fresh oregano or |
| 6 garlic cloves, chopped | 1 teaspoon dried |
| 3 medium tomatoes, peeled, seeded and chopped* | 1/8 teaspoon nutmeg |
| 1 cup water | 3 large carrots, sliced |
| 1/2 cup dry white wine | 3/4 lb. fresh green beans, trimmed, cut into 1 1/2-inch pieces |

1. Heat oil in large saucepot or Dutch oven over medium-high heat until hot. Add beef; cook until browned, adding salt and pepper to taste. When almost browned, add onions and garlic to cook with beef.
2. Add all remaining ingredients except carrots and green beans; mix well. Bring to a boil. Reduce heat; cover and simmer 1 hour or until beef is tender.
3. Add carrots; simmer 20 minutes. Add green beans; simmer an additional 10 minutes or until vegetables are tender. Season to taste with salt and pepper. Serve with wrinkled potatoes or French bread.

*See page 35.

4 to 6 servings

It's important to eat good food, important that our families and those who join us at the table are satisfied.

# Salsa de Carne y Tomate

## Meat and Tomato Sauce for Pasta

*Ruth Lozano Rodriquez*

"Our cuisine is getting more creative, due partly to the influence of tourists. Traditional cooking is excellent, but there are also other things, no? In the olden days, the cuisine was more stews, vegetables, a little bay leaf. Now, foods are prepared with more spices, with things that aren't customary. Today we're becoming more gourmet."

| | |
|---|---|
| 1 lb. ground beef | 1/2 cup dry white wine |
| 1 large onion, sliced | 1 tablespoon fresh thyme leaves |
| 3 garlic cloves, finely chopped | 1 teaspoon salt |
| 2 tablespoons extra virgin olive oil | 1/2 teaspoon paprika |
| 5 medium tomatoes, peeled and chopped, | 1/4 teaspoon freshly ground pepper |
|   or halved and grated* | 12 oz. spaghetti or linguine |

1. In large skillet over medium-high heat, cook ground beef, onion and garlic until beef is thoroughly cooked and onion is transparent, stirring frequently. Drain if necessary. (If ground beef is very lean, add 1 tablespoon of the oil when cooking beef.)
2. Stir in oil, tomatoes, wine, thyme, salt, paprika and pepper. Bring to a boil. Reduce heat; simmer, uncovered, 15 minutes, stirring occasionally.
3. Meanwhile, cook spaghetti according to package directions, or until it is al dente; drain. Serve with meat and tomato sauce.

*See page 35.

4 servings

A mild sauce with an extra zing of wine.

# Calamares en Su Tinta

## Squid in Its Own Ink

| | |
|---|---|
| 2 lb. squid | 2 tablespoons chopped fresh parsley |
| 2 medium onions, finely chopped | 1 teaspoon coarse salt |
| 1 medium red bell pepper, cut into thin strips | 1 tablespoon olive oil |
| | Squid ink* |
| 2 cups dry white wine | 1 teaspoon sugar |
| 4 garlic cloves, chopped | |

1. Rinse squid; slice if large size. Place in large saucepan or Dutch oven. Add onions, bell pepper and wine.
2. In food processor or with mortar and pestle, process garlic, parsley, salt and oil. Stir into saucepan. Bring to a boil. Reduce heat; cook uncovered, 5 minutes.
3. Cover and simmer 45 minutes or until squid is tender.
4. Mix squid ink with sugar. Stir into squid mixture.

*Squid ink can be found at specialty food stores or fish markets. The squid ink will turn the sauce a black color. For this recipe, a 0.3-oz. package was used.

4 to 6 servings

In creative cooking, wine is very important ... there are other things than just potatoes and mojo!

COOK

# Papas Viudas

## Widowed Potatoes

*Candelaria Hernández Linares (Lala)*

"My parents had a 'pension,' a guest house, for their whole life. I continued with it until '97. Although this isn't a town with much tourism, there have always been people who have stayed and come back again. ... In the old days salted fish was the basic food. When people didn't have a lot of money they bought salt fish almost every day; very little meat was eaten. Today more meat is eaten and it's almost cheaper than fish."

*1 tablespoon olive oil*

*2 garlic cloves, finely chopped*

*4 medium red or Yukon gold potatoes, peeled, cut into 3/4-inch cubes*

*1 1/2 teaspoons salt*

*1/2 cup dry white wine*

*1 cup chopped fresh parsley*

1. Heat oil in medium saucepan over medium heat until hot. Add garlic; sauté until tender.
2. Add potatoes, salt, wine and enough water to almost cover potatoes. Bring to a boil. Reduce heat; cover and simmer about 15 minutes or until potatoes are tender. Drain; stir in parsley.

4 servings

The name? I don't know, it could be because they're alone, just garlic and parsley. Widowed Potatoes can be eaten plain or with fried eggs.

# Pescado en Escabeche

## Pickled Fish

| **Fish** | **1 medium tomato, peeled, chopped**** |
|---|---|
| 1 1/2 lb. fish fillets (such as cod, halibut or haddock) | 3 tablespoons slivered almonds |
| 2 tablespoons olive oil | 3 tablespoons raisins |
| Salt and freshly ground pepper | 1 cup dry white wine |
| | 1/2 cup water |
| **Escabeche** | 2 tablespoons white wine vinegar or sherry vinegar |
| 1/4 cup olive oil | 1 teaspoon salt |
| 1 medium onion, sliced | 1 teaspoon paprika |
| 8 garlic cloves, peeled* | 2 bay leaves |

1. Rinse fish fillets; pat dry. Heat 2 tablespoons oil in large skillet over medium heat until hot. Add fish; cook until lightly browned and fish flakes easily with fork. Arrange fish in single layer in deep glass or ceramic casserole. Season to taste with salt and pepper.
2. Heat 1/4 cup oil in same skillet over medium heat until hot. Add onion; sauté until softened but not browned. Add garlic, tomato, almonds and raisins; sauté a few minutes. Stir in all remaining ingredients. Bring to a boil. Reduce heat; simmer, uncovered, 5 minutes, stirring occasionally.
3. Pour over fish in casserole. Cover tightly; refrigerate up to 4 days. Remove bay leaves before serving. Serve chilled.

*To peel garlic easily, lightly press clove with side of chef's knife. Peel should slip off.

**See page 35.

4 to 6 servings

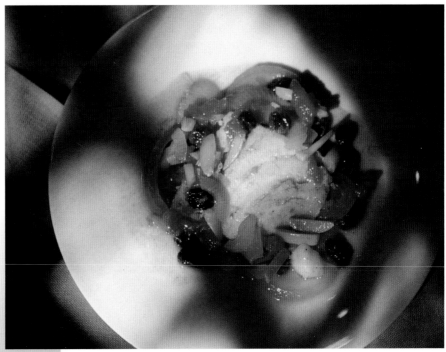

This is a Holy Week recipe. It's very old. Today almost nobody makes it; fried food is more popular. A long time ago when we made it, there were no refrigerators and it lasted for three or four days.

# Mojo Colorado

## Garlicky Red Sauce

1/2 head garlic (8 to 10 cloves), peeled, coarsely chopped*
1/4 cup bread crumbs
1 tablespoon paprika
1/2 teaspoon salt
1/2 teaspoon cumin
3/4 cup extra virgin olive oil
1/2 cup water
1/4 cup red wine vinegar

1. In food processor or with mortar and pestle, process garlic, bread crumbs, paprika, salt and cumin.
2. Add oil, water and vinegar; blend until smooth. Serve with potatoes, fish or chicken dishes.
*To peel garlic easily, lightly press clove with side of chef's knife. Peel should slip off.

Makes 1 1/2 cups

Taster

Ahh-mazing! Bottle and patent this.

# Mojo Verde

## Parsley Sauce

*1 cup chopped fresh parsley*

*3 or 4 garlic cloves, peeled*

*1 teaspoon salt*

*1/2 teaspoon cumin*

*1/2 cup extra virgin olive oil*

*3 tablespoons white wine vinegar*

*1 tablespoon water*

1. In food processor or with mortar and pestle, process parsley, garlic, salt and cumin.

2. Add oil, vinegar and water; blend well. Serve with fish, steamed vegetables or for dunking bread.

Makes 1 cup

The best! Works well
with potatoes.

Taster

# Conejo en Salmorejo

## Braised Rabbit in Pepper and Herb Sauce

*Carlos Gamonal Jiménez*
*Mesón El Drago, El Socorro, Tegueste, Tenerife*

"Because I worked a long time in France and other countries, it's natural that I use a little of these cuisines. It helps me renew our own gastronomy. We respect the local cuisine, the cuisine of the earth—watercress stews, marinated rabbit, goat, boiled dinner. We try to give these dishes the worth they deserve. In the end it is our culture."

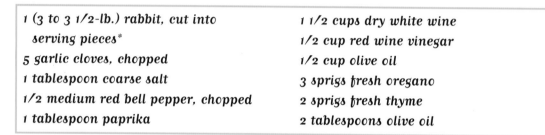

1 (3 to 3 1/2-lb.) rabbit, cut into serving pieces*

5 garlic cloves, chopped

1 tablespoon coarse salt

1/2 medium red bell pepper, chopped

1 tablespoon paprika

1 1/2 cups dry white wine

1/2 cup red wine vinegar

1/2 cup olive oil

3 sprigs fresh oregano

2 sprigs fresh thyme

2 tablespoons olive oil

1. Place rabbit pieces in large shallow glass dish or resealable plastic bag.
2. In food processor or with mortar and pestle, process garlic, salt, bell pepper and paprika until very fine. Gradually add wine, vinegar and 1/2 cup oil in thin stream, processing until well blended. Pour over rabbit. Arrange oregano and thyme among rabbit pieces. Cover dish or seal bag; refrigerate several hours or overnight to marinate.
3. Drain rabbit pieces, reserving marinade. Heat 2 tablespoons oil in large skillet over medium-high heat until hot. Add rabbit pieces; cook 10 minutes or until all sides are well browned. Remove rabbit from skillet.
4. Add marinade to same skillet. Bring to a boil. Reduce heat; simmer, uncovered, 10 minutes.
5. Return rabbit to skillet; bring to a boil. Reduce heat; cover and simmer about 1 hour or until rabbit is tender. Serve rabbit with sauce and Papas Arrugadas, page 214.

*This dish can also be made with chicken.

4 to 6 servings

Canarian cuisine has always been very aromatic, with rosemary, bay, thyme, mint, all these herbs. You can't have a salmorejo without them. They're things we use a lot in our cooking, and we're incorporating new ones like basil that the Italians brought, also flavorful.

# *Bocinegro Canario*

## Canary Island Fish Stew

### *Fish Broth**
1 lb. fish bones
4 cups water
1/2 cup dry white wine
2 tablespoons olive oil
1 medium tomato, quartered
1 small onion, quartered
1 medium red bell pepper, quartered
1 teaspoon salt
1/4 teaspoon whole peppercorns
1/4 teaspoon saffron

### *Sofrito*
3 tablespoons olive oil
1 medium onion, chopped
2 medium tomatoes, peeled, chopped**
1 medium red bell pepper, chopped

### *Stew*
1/2 cup dry white wine
4 cups fish broth
8 medium red potatoes
Salt and freshly ground pepper
2 tablespoons chopped fresh
   parsley or cilantro
1 tablespoon chopped garlic
1 teaspoon coarse salt
1/2 teaspoon saffron

### *Fish*
2 lb. firm white fish fillets (such as
   porgy, halibut or snapper)

1. To make fish broth, combine all fish broth ingredients except saffron in large saucepan. Bring to a boil. Reduce heat; skim off foam. Add saffron; simmer, uncovered, 30 minutes. Cool broth slightly. Strain.
2. To make sofrito, heat 3 tablespoons oil in large soup pot over medium heat until hot. Add onion; sauté until softened. Add tomatoes and bell pepper; cook until softened, stirring occasionally.
3. Add 1/2 cup wine to sofrito; simmer about 10 minutes or until almost completely reduced. Add 4 cups fish broth. Bring to a boil. Reduce heat; cook uncovered, 10 minutes.
4. Meanwhile, peel and cube potatoes. Add potatoes to soup pot after fish broth has simmered 10 minutes. Cook potatoes about 10 minutes. Season to taste with salt and pepper.
5. In food processor or with mortar and pestle, process parsley, garlic, coarse salt and saffron.
6. Add fish to soup pot; top with parsley and garlic mixture. Cover; cook 15 minutes or until potatoes are tender and fish flakes easily with fork.

*Fish broth recipe can be doubled. Freeze extra for other recipes.
**See page 35.

6 servings

I believe Canarian cuisine is one
of the healthiest in the world.

# Puchero Canario

## Canary Island Meat and Vegetable Stew

| | |
|---|---|
| 1 1/2 cups dried garbanzo beans | 1 sweet potato, peeled, cut into large pieces |
| 1 (1-lb.) beef soup bone | 1/2 to 3/4 lb. winter squash, peeled, cubed* |
| 1 lb. pork shoulder | 3 garlic cloves, peeled |
| 1 medium onion, coarsely chopped | 1 teaspoon saffron |
| 2 large carrots, cut into thick slices | 1/4 cup chopped fresh cilantro or parsley |
| 1 tablespoon salt | 1/2 lb. fresh green beans |
| Water | 1 medium zucchini, cut into 1/2-inch-thick slices |
| 1/2 lb. chorizo, sliced | |
| 1/2 lb. green cabbage, chopped (about 4 cups) | 1 Bosc pear, cut into pieces |
| 2 medium red potatoes, cut into large pieces | 2 ears of corn, cut into 2-inch-thick slices |

1. Soak beans overnight in water to cover. Drain just before using.
2. In large soup pot or Dutch oven, combine drained beans, beef bone, pork shoulder, onion, carrots and salt. Add enough water to cover meat and vegetables. Bring to a boil; skim off foam. Reduce heat; cover and simmer 1 hour.
3. Remove beef bone and pork shoulder from soup pot. Remove meat from bones; return meat to soup pot.
4. Add chorizo, cabbage, potatoes, sweet potato and squash. Return to a boil. Reduce heat; simmer 15 minutes.
5. Meanwhile, in food processor or with mortar and pestle, process garlic, saffron and cilantro. Add to stew.
6. Add green beans, zucchini, pear and corn. Return to a boil. Cover; simmer 15 minutes or until all vegetables are tender. If desired, serve with Mojo de Cilantro, page 209.

*To make squash easier to peel, heat in microwave for several minutes. Cool slightly, peel.

8 to 10 servings

We have a lot here from America: sugar cane, potatoes, corn, avocados, mango, papaya, yucca, pears, peppers, bananas. Before all this came, there weren't many exotic fruits here.

# *Mojo de Cilantro*

## Cilantro Sauce

*3 or 4 garlic cloves, peeled*
*1 teaspoon salt*
*1 medium green bell pepper, chopped*
*1 cup chopped fresh cilantro*
*2/3 cup extra virgin olive oil*
*1/4 cup wine vinegar*

1. In food processor or with mortar and pestle, process garlic and salt. Add bell pepper and cilantro; process.
2. Add oil and vinegar; blend well.

Makes 2 cups

A perfect sauce for fish, fresh
cheese or steamed vegetables;
wonderful for brushing on
chicken or seafood on the grill.

# Mojo Picón

## Spicy Sauce

> *2 dried chiles (such as Spanish ñoras or New Mexico style)*
> *1/4 cup red wine vinegar*
> *6 to 8 garlic cloves, peeled*
> *1 teaspoon cumin*
> *1/2 teaspoon salt*
> *1 cup extra virgin olive oil*
> *2 tablespoons paprika*

1. Break chiles into pieces; soak in vinegar for at least 45 minutes.
2. Drain chiles, reserving vinegar. Remove seeds and stems; finely chop chiles.
3. In food processor or with mortar and pestle, process garlic, cumin and salt. Add chiles and reserved vinegar; continue processing until no large pieces remain.
4. Add oil and paprika; blend well.

Makes 1 1/2 cups

Try this on tortillas and other egg dishes, or as a piquant marinade.

# *Huevos Rellenos con Atún*

## Tuna-Stuffed Eggs

*María Candelaria Guanche Cuba (Yaya)*

"I like to cook; it's what I like to do most in the house, but it takes a lot of time. There's no way to avoid it because everything has its cooking time. ... Two of these recipes are from my sister, Luz Marina Guanche Cuba."

**6 hard-cooked eggs, peeled**

**1 (6-oz.) can tuna in olive oil, drained**

**1/3 cup mayonnaise**

**2 tablespoons finely chopped onion**

**1/4 to 1/2 teaspoon salt**

**2 tablespoons finely chopped fresh parsley or cilantro**

1. Cut each egg in half lengthwise. Remove yolks; place in small bowl. Mash yolks with fork.
2. Stir in tuna, mayonnaise, onion, salt and 1 tablespoon of the parsley.
3. Fill egg whites with tuna mixture. Sprinkle with remaining tablespoon parsley.*

*Any remaining tuna mixture can be used as a sandwich spread.

6 servings

When we invite people, when there are little savory tidbits, there are almost always stuffed eggs. We make them a lot.

# Croquetas de Pescado

## Crispy Fish Croquettes

1 tablespoon olive oil

1/2 medium onion, chopped

2 tablespoons butter

1/3 cup flour

1 cup milk

1 1/2 lb. firm white fish (such as cod, snapper or halibut), cooked, flaked; or leftover fish (about 2 cups)

4 teaspoons chopped fresh parsley

3/4 teaspoons salt

2 eggs

1 teaspoon water

Bread crumbs

Olive oil for frying

1. Heat 1 tablespoon oil in heavy medium saucepan over medium heat until hot. Add onion; cook about 10 minutes or until golden, stirring occasionally.
2. Stir in butter until melted. Stir in flour; cook and stir 1 minute. Gradually add milk, stirring constantly. Bring to a boil. Stir in fish, parsley and 1/2 teaspoon of the salt. Remove from heat; refrigerate 3 to 4 hours or until firm.
3. Dipping hands in water, shape chilled fish mixture into small egg-like shapes.
4. In small bowl, combine eggs, water and remaining 1/4 teaspoon salt; beat well. Place bread crumbs in shallow dish. Dip shaped fish mixture in beaten eggs; coat with bread crumbs, pressing crumbs into mixture.
5. Heat 3/4 inch of oil in skillet or saucepan over high heat until very hot. Fry croquettes 1 to 2 minutes or until golden brown on both sides. Remove from skillet; drain on paper towels. If desired, keep warm in 200°F. oven for up to 30 minutes.

6 servings

You have to keep stirring the sauce so it doesn't get lumpy. When you fry the croquettes, the oil should cover them by half so one side doesn't get done more than the other.

Cocinero COOK

# Conejo con Cebolla

## Braised Rabbit with Onions

| Rabbit | Marinade | Sofrito |
|---|---|---|
| 1 (3 to 3 1/2-lb.) rabbit, cut into serving pieces* | 1 cup dry white wine | 2 tablespoons olive oil |
| 1 tablespoon olive oil | 1/2 cup olive oil | 2 medium onions, chopped |
| Flour | 1 teaspoon salt | 1 medium red bell pepper, chopped |
| | Small handful fresh thyme leaves | 1 medium tomato, peeled, seeded and chopped*** |
| | Small handful fresh oregano leaves | |
| | 1 small head garlic, separated into cloves, peeled** | |
| | 1 bay leaf | |

1. Place rabbit pieces in large shallow glass dish or resealable plastic bag. Combine all marinade ingredients; pour over rabbit. Cover dish or seal bag; refrigerate at least 2 hours or overnight, turning rabbit pieces at least once.
2. To make sofrito, heat 2 tablespoons oil in large saucepot or Dutch oven over medium heat until hot. Add onions; sauté until softened. Add bell pepper and tomato; cook until softened, stirring occasionally. Set aside.
3. Remove rabbit pieces from marinade; drain and pat dry. Place marinade in medium saucepan; bring to a boil. Boil, uncovered, 10 minutes to reduce.
4. Heat 1 tablespoon oil in large skillet over medium-high heat until hot. Dust rabbit pieces with flour; add to hot oil in skillet; cook for about 10 minutes or until all sides of rabbit pieces are well browned.
5. Add browned rabbit and boiled marinade to sofrito mixture in saucepot. Bring to a boil. Reduce heat; cover and simmer 1 hour or until rabbit is tender. Remove bay leaf before serving.

*This dish can also be made with chicken.

**To peel garlic easily, lightly press clove with side of chef's knife. Peel should slip off.

***See page 35.

4 to 6 servings

The garlic from here is more flavorful, not as strong as the garlic from elsewhere, though sometimes I don't buy what we have here. It's so small, it's infuriating when it has to be peeled.

# Papas Arrugadas

## Wrinkled Potatoes

*2 lb. small potatoes (1 1/2 to 2 inches in diameter), scrubbed*
*2 cups kosher salt or coarse sea salt*

1. In large saucepot, place potatoes and enough water to cover potatoes by 1 inch. Stir in salt.
2. Bring to a boil. Reduce heat to low; partially cover and simmer 20 minutes or until tender. Drain; leave potatoes in saucepot.
3. Keep potatoes warm over low heat, shaking saucepot occasionally. Potatoes should be dry and slightly wrinkled.
4. To serve, let guests peel their own potatoes.

8 servings

I never cover the pot after
the potatoes are drained
because they 'sweat' and then
won't stay salted. It's very
rare that you go to a house
where there are Canarians and
they don't have wrinkled
potatoes. We use them with
everything-fish, meat, everything.

# Carne de Cabra Arreglada

## Goat Stew with Fresh Herbs

### Marinade

2 medium red bell peppers

1/2 to 3/4 head garlic, separated into
   cloves, peeled*

1/2 cup fresh thyme leaves

1/2 cup fresh oregano leaves

1 teaspoon salt

3 cups dry white wine

1 cup water

1/2 cup olive oil

3 bay leaves

### Goat

2 lb. goat meat, cut up**

Freshly ground pepper and salt

Chopped fresh parsley

1. In food processor, finely chop bell peppers, garlic, thyme, oregano and 1 teaspoon salt. In large glass baking dish or resealable plastic bag, combine bell pepper mixture with all remaining marinade ingredients.
2. Add goat meat; stir to cover with marinade. Sprinkle with freshly ground pepper; mix well. Cover dish or seal bag; refrigerate overnight to marinate.
3. Place goat meat and marinade in large soup pot or Dutch oven. Bring to a boil. Skim off fat; cover. Reduce heat; simmer 2 1/2 to 3 hours or until meat is tender. Add extra water or wine while cooking to keep meat covered. Season to taste with salt and pepper. Serve goat meat sprinkled with parsley.

*To peel garlic easily, lightly press clove with side of chef's knife. Peel should slip off.

**Goat meat can be found in Middle Eastern meat markets. Ask the butcher to cut up the meat for stew. This dish can also be made with lamb.

6 servings

I have thyme in my garden.
There's a lot of oregano in the
hills. I bring it home and dry it
in the sun on the roof terrace.
The flavor of wild oregano is
much better.

Thyme plant, Tenerife

# Mojo de Queso

## Cheese Sauce (from Luz Marina Guanche Cuba)

*1/2 medium green bell pepper*
*2 garlic cloves, peeled*
*1/4 teaspoon cumin*
*Dash salt*
*2 cups freshly grated Parmesan or Manchego cheese*
*1/2 cup water*
*1/2 cup extra virgin olive oil*

1. In food processor or with mortar and pestle, chop bell pepper, garlic, cumin and salt. Add cheese; blend well.
2. Slowly add water and oil until of desired consistency.

Makes 2 cups

Try this with potatoes, crackers or bread; or as a dip for fresh vegetables.

# Guisantes Tenerife

## Peas Tenerife (from Luz Marina Guanche Cuba)

| | |
|---|---|
| 2 tablespoons olive oil | 1/2 teaspoon salt |
| 1 large tomato, chopped | 1 bay leaf |
| 1 medium onion, chopped | 1 (1-lb.) pkg. frozen peas |
| 1/2 medium green bell pepper, chopped | 1/2 cup water |
| 2 garlic cloves, chopped | 4 hard-cooked eggs, peeled, cut into |
| 2 tablespoons chopped fresh parsley | wedges, if desired |
| 1 teaspoon fresh thyme leaves or | |
| 1/2 teaspoon dried | |

1. Heat oil in large skillet over medium heat until hot. Add tomato, onion, bell pepper, garlic, parsley, thyme, salt and bay leaf; sauté until softened.
2. Add peas and water; cover and cook 6 to 8 minutes or until peas are tender. Drain; remove bay leaf. Serve garnished with eggs.

4 to 6 servings

This was unique, fresh-tasting.

Romería de San Marco, Tegueste

One spring weekend in Tenerife in the Canary
Islands, the season's first Romeria, or
religious festival, was taking place. Visitors
came from far and wide to participate, many
in traditional dress. Different groups
representing trades or professions—meats,
cutlery, wine, milling, etc., had decorated
wooden carts using seeds and grains. As the
ox-drawn carts moved through the town, people
on top threw food to the assembled crowd—
wrinkled potatoes, meats, sweets. Those lucky
enough to be standing close by got a hastily-
poured glass of wine as well. As María
Candelaria (Yaya) told me, 'The Romerías
begin in April with San Marco in Tegueste and
end with San Benito in July. Some people go
to them all and don't lose a one. I believe
the best carts are at the festival of San
Marco; they work for months making them.'

# *Potaje de Verduras*

## Vegetable Stew

*Dolores Morales Méndez (Lola)*

"I cook like my mother did, and like the woman who taught me. She was as good as a professional, and wrote several cookbooks. Before I married, I worked in her house and learned from her. Now I cook for two homes. I make two, three, as many as five meals, and put them in their freezer."

| | |
|---|---|
| 1 tablespoon olive oil | 1/2 medium head green cabbage, |
| 1 medium onion, chopped | coarsely chopped (about 5 cups) |
| 1 garlic clove, chopped | 1 bay leaf |
| 2 cups chicken broth | 2 medium zucchini, sliced |
| 2 medium carrots, sliced | 1/2 lb. fresh green beans |
| 1/2 lb. winter squash, peeled, cubed* | Salt and freshly ground pepper |

1. Heat oil in large saucepan or Dutch oven over medium heat until hot. Add onion; sauté until softened. Add garlic; sauté an additional few minutes.
2. Add chicken broth, carrots, squash, cabbage and bay leaf. Bring to a boil. Reduce heat; cover and simmer 15 minutes.
3. Add zucchini and green beans; simmer about 5 minutes or until vegetables are tender. Remove bay leaf before serving. Season to taste with salt and pepper.

*To make squash easier to peel, heat in microwave for several minutes. Cool slightly; peel.

6 servings

Cooking today is 'less time,' because we can't work at it all day. Before, a lot of time was spent in the kitchen ... a lot, a lot, a lot.

# Frangollo

## Cornmeal Pudding with Raisins and Almonds

| | |
|---|---|
| 4 oz. (3/4 cup) whole blanched almonds, lightly toasted* | 2 tablespoons butter |
| 2 cups whole milk | 2 egg yolks |
| 1 cup cornmeal | 1/4 teaspoon salt |
| 1/2 cup raisins | 1 cinnamon stick |
| 1/3 cup sugar | Peel from 1/2 lemon, cut into thin slivers |

1. Reserve 1/4 cup toasted whole almonds for garnish; in food processor, grind remaining 1/2 cup almonds.
2. In medium saucepan, combine ground almonds and all remaining ingredients; cook over medium heat about 10 minutes or until pudding thickens, stirring constantly.
3. Remove cinnamon stick. Spoon into serving dish. Garnish top with reserved whole almonds.

*To toast nuts, see page 232.

6 to 8 servings

This is a typical Canarian dish. It's ground corn. Now they sell it as a dessert, but before, in the time of the Spanish Civil War, it was a main meal because they didn't have anything else.

COCINERO COOK

# Mojo de Azafrán

## Saffron Sauce

*María Ysidora de León Guanche (Dora)*

"In the fall, at the time of the grape harvest, neighbors and nearby families get together to pick the grapes and then to eat. The typical harvest meal is salted fish, wrinkled potatoes with the skin, gofio, the wine that's left from the previous year, and saffron mojo. However, this tradition is getting lost because of new harvesting technologies."

| | |
|---|---|
| 2 tablespoons saffron | Dash freshly ground pepper |
| 1/2 medium red bell pepper, chopped | 1/4 cup extra virgin olive oil |
| 1 garlic clove, chopped | 1/2 teaspoon red wine vinegar |
| 1/2 teaspoon coarse salt | 2 tablespoons water or to taste |

1. To bring out flavor of saffron, warm on lid of cooking pot or in small skillet over very low heat just before crumbling.
2. In food processor or with mortar and pestle, process saffron, bell pepper, garlic, salt and pepper.
3. Add oil and vinegar; blend well. Slowly add water until of desired consistency. Serve with meat and fish dishes.

Makes 3/4 cup

Saffron is a lot of work to gather. If we were to compare the harvesting to the cost of the saffron, we would find that the work is very poorly paid. Mojo is typically Canarian.

# Sopa Verde

## Green Egg Soup

8 (3/4-inch-thick) slices day-old
  baguette, cubed
4 tablespoons olive oil
1 medium onion, chopped
2 garlic cloves, chopped
8 medium red potatoes, peeled, cubed
2 teaspoons salt
1 teaspoon fresh thyme leaves or
  1/2 teaspoon dried

1/4 teaspoon saffron
Water
1/2 cup chopped fresh parsley
3 eggs, beaten
Salt and freshly ground pepper

1. Heat 2 tablespoons of the oil in large saucepan or Dutch oven over medium heat until hot. Add bread cubes to saucepan; cook until golden brown. Remove bread cubes; set aside.
2. Add remaining 2 tablespoons oil to saucepan. Add onion and garlic; sauté over medium heat until softened.
3. Add potatoes, 2 teaspoons salt, thyme and saffron; add just enough water to cover (about 4 cups). Bring to a boil. Reduce heat; cover and simmer about 30 minutes or until potatoes are tender.
4. Towards end of cooking, add parsley. Pour eggs into soup, stirring constantly. Broth will change color and thicken. Season to taste with salt and pepper.
5. Divide bread cubes into individual soup bowls. Add soup.

6 servings

This would make a perfect meal on a snowy afternoon.

# Albóndigas de Dora

## Dora's Meatballs

### Sauce

2 tablespoons olive oil

1 medium onion, chopped

1 medium carrot, chopped

1 medium red bell pepper, chopped

4 garlic cloves, chopped

1 teaspoon salt

1/2 teaspoon dried oregano

1/2 teaspoon dried thyme

1/4 teaspoon pepper

1/8 teaspoon nutmeg

1 bay leaf

1 cup water

1/2 cup dry white wine

### Meatballs

2 lb. lean ground beef

1 1/2 cups bread crumbs

2 tablespoons chopped fresh parsley

1 1/2 teaspoons salt

1 teaspoon dried oregano

3 eggs

Flour

2 tablespoons olive oil

1. Heat 2 tablespoons oil in medium skillet over medium heat until hot. Add all sauce ingredients except water and wine; cook until vegetables are softened, stirring frequently.
2. Cool sauce slightly. Remove bay leaf. In food processor or blender, purée sauce.
3. Meanwhile, in medium bowl, combine ground beef, bread crumbs, parsley, 1 1/2 teaspoons salt, 1 teaspoon oregano and eggs; mix well. Shape into balls, using about 1/4 cup mixture for each meatball. Coat lightly with flour.
4. Heat 2 tablespoons oil in large skillet over medium-high heat until hot. Brown meatballs on all sides in hot oil.
5. Stir in sauce, water and wine. Bring to a boil. Reduce heat; cover and simmer about 15 minutes or until meatballs are thoroughly cooked and sauce is heated. Serve meatballs with sauce.

8 servings

The meatballs can be eaten with bread, and with French fries or peas. ... I like to cook. I learned with my mother and my grandmother.

## Flan de Huevos

### Classic Flan

12 tablespoons sugar
1 teaspoon water
5 eggs
2 cups whole milk
1/8 teaspoon cinnamon

1. Heat oven to 350°F. Caramelize sugar by placing 6 tablespoons of the sugar and water in heavy, medium skillet or saucepan. (Adding water will help sugar melt more evenly.) Heat over medium heat, stirring constantly with heat-resistant spoon, until sugar is melted and becomes golden.
2. Immediately pour caramelized sugar into shallow baking dish, such as 9-inch pie plate, or shallow mold. (Work quickly and carefully, using potholders, as caramel will make baking dish become extremely hot. It is okay if caramelized sugar does not cover entire bottom of dish; it will melt as flan bakes.)
3. Lightly beat eggs in medium bowl with wire whisk. Stir in remaining 6 tablespoons sugar, milk and cinnamon. Pour over caramelized sugar in baking dish. Place dish in shallow pan of hot water.
4. Bake 25 to 35 minutes or until knife inserted in center comes out clean. Cool. Cover; refrigerate until serving time. (Flan can be made a day ahead.)
5. To serve, run knife around edge of baking dish; invert flan onto shallow serving plate.

6 servings

Cooking is evolving. They're introducing foods from other countries as a way to find variety and try new things. But thanks to the traditional celebrations, all our recipes aren't lost. Egg flan is a delicious dessert that's nutritious too.

It always paid to ask. When I discovered something I liked, a recipe that nobody had given me, I found that waiters, bartenders, and nearby diners were only too happy to weigh in. I spent many meals at the bar, tasting, watching, listening and finding out how. The bar is a great vantage point for learning about food.

# Ensalada de Pulpo

## Octopus Salad

### Salad
3/4 to 1 lb. octopus (1 large or 2 small)*

1 medium green bell pepper,
  coarsely chopped

1 medium onion, coarsely chopped

1 medium tomato, coarsely chopped

1/4 cup roasted red bell pepper, chopped

### Dressing
1/4 cup extra virgin olive oil

2 tablespoons lemon juice

1/2 teaspoon salt

1. Prepare octopus as directed in Pulpo a la Gallega recipe, page 74. When cooked and cooled, cut body and tentacles into bite-sized pieces; place in medium salad bowl.
2. Add all remaining salad ingredients; toss gently. Refrigerate to chill.
3. In small bowl, combine all dressing ingredients; blend well. Pour over salad; mix gently.

*This salad can also be made with any mix of cooked seafood.

6 to 8 servings

From a chef: Octopus is usually frozen before cooking. If it's fresh you have to pound it 33 times with a stick or against the floor, if not it comes out hard. Once it's been frozen it's ready to cook.

# *Salmorejo Cordobés*

## Thick Gazpacho from Córdoba

| | |
|---|---|
| 4 cups (1-inch) bread cubes from Italian or French bread | 1 teaspoon salt |
| Water | 2 teaspoons red wine vinegar |
| 3 medium tomatoes, peeled, seeded and chopped* | 1/4 cup extra virgin olive oil |
| 2 garlic cloves, chopped | 2 hard-cooked eggs, peeled, diced |
| | 1/4 cup diced ham |

1. Cover bread with water; soak for several minutes.
2. In food processor or blender, process tomatoes, garlic, salt and vinegar.
3. Squeeze water from bread. Gradually add bread and oil to mixture in food processor; process until smooth. Divide into individual bowls. Garnish with eggs and ham.

*See page 35.

4 servings

I discovered this in a bar in Córdoba, where Salmorejo is an art. It is sometimes garnished with chopped red pepper. Salmorejo is thick enough to eat with a fork.

# Sardinas con Pimiento Rojo

## Sardines with Roasted Peppers

*8 (3/8-inch-thick) slices baguette*

*Sardines*

*1 roasted red bell pepper, cut into 16 slices\**

*Chopped fresh parsley*

*Extra virgin olive oil*

1. Top each baguette slice with 1 or 2 sardines and 2 small slices roasted pepper.
2. Sprinkle each with parsley; drizzle with oil.

\*If using bottled peppers, drain well and dry on paper towels; cut into 16 slices.

8 tapas

Nice balance between salty sardine and sweet red pepper!

Taster

## *Queso Fresco con Membrillo*

### Fresh Cheese with Quince Paste

*8 (3/8-inch-thick) slices baguette*

*8 thin slices plain soft white cheese (such as fresh mozzarella or queso blanco), cut to fit baguette slices*

*8 thin slices quince paste, cut slightly smaller than cheese*

Top each baguette slice with 1 cheese slice and 1 slice of quince paste.

8 tapas

Pair with spicy tapas.

# Naranjas con Aceite de Oliva

## Oranges in Olive Oil

**2 medium oranges**

**3 tablespoons extra virgin olive oil**

**1/4 teaspoon coarse salt**

1. Peel oranges. Cut into bite-sized pieces; place in medium serving bowl.
2. Drizzle with oil. Sprinkle with salt.

4 servings

I tasted this at the international food show, Feria Alimentaria 2000, in Barcelona. It was served as a way to taste olive oil, but was too delicious (and easy!) not to pass on.

# Tapa Gitana

## Gypsy-Style Tapa

| **Salad** | **Dressing** |
|---|---|
| 2 oranges, peeled, sliced | 1/4 cup extra virgin olive oil |
| 1/2 medium onion, thinly sliced into rings | 1 teaspoon red wine vinegar or sherry vinegar |
| 12 sardines, drained | 1 teaspoon salt |
| 1/4 cup black olives (such as kalamata or oil-cured) | |

1. Divide orange and onion slices onto individual plates. Top with sardines and olives.
2. In small bowl, combine all dressing ingredients; blend well. Drizzle on top.

4 servings

This was inspired by a slide I saw at a lecture on Gypsy Cooking at La Caixa in Barcelona. It pictured a platter of orange slices, onion rings and sardines. In the background, a song was playing— "Me lo como todo, I eat it all up."

# Ensalada de Tomate

## Tomato Salad with Hazelnuts

2 medium tomatoes, seeded, cut into
   bite-sized pieces

1/2 cup cubed white cheese (such as
   fresh mozzarella or queso blanco)

1/4 cup black olives (such as kalamata
   or oil-cured)

1/4 cup hazelnuts, toasted, skin removed*

1/4 cup extra virgin olive oil

1 to 2 tablespoons red or white wine vinegar

1/2 teaspoon salt

1. In serving bowl, combine tomatoes, cheese and olives. Sprinkle with hazelnuts.
2. Mix oil, vinegar and salt. Drizzle over salad.

*To toast nuts, place on cookie sheet; bake at 350°F. for about 8 minutes, turning frequently to avoid scorching. If
  unblanched, remove skins by rubbing nuts together in towel.

4 servings

At Beltran, in Barcelona, where
they sell prepared foods, a
wonderful salad similar to this
led me to experiment.

# *Solomillo en Escabeche*

## Marinated Pork Tenderloin

| | |
|---|---|
| 1 to 2 tablespoons olive oil | Salt and freshly ground pepper |
| 2 garlic cloves, quartered | 1/2 cup olive oil |
| 1 (3/4 to 1-lb.) pork tenderloin | 1/4 cup red wine vinegar |
| 1 1/2 teaspoon whole peppercorns, bruised | |

1. Heat 1 to 2 tablespoons oil in large skillet over medium heat until hot. Add garlic; cook until browned. Remove garlic from skillet; reserve garlic.
2. Increase heat to medium-high; add tenderloin and bruised peppercorns. Brown tenderloin on all sides; season to taste with salt and pepper. Reduce heat; cover and cook 5 to 10 minutes or until tenderloin is slightly pink in center (150 to 155°F.), turning frequently.
3. In small bowl, combine 1/2 cup oil and vinegar. Add to skillet with reserved garlic; bring to a boil. Reduce heat to low; simmer 5 minutes. Serve pork tenderloin with garlic and peppercorn sauce.

4 servings

I discovered this at a party and
loved it!

# Patatas a lo Pobre

## Humble Potatoes

*1 tablespoon olive oil*
*1 medium onion, chopped*
*1 large green bell pepper, diced*
*4 medium baking potatoes, thickly sliced*
*1 teaspoon salt*
*Water*

1. Heat oil in medium saucepan over medium heat until hot. Add onion and bell pepper; sauté several minutes.
2. Add potatoes, salt and water to barely cover vegetables. Bring to a boil. Reduce heat; cover and simmer 10 to 15 minutes or until potatoes are tender.
3. Drain. Serve potato mixture with Mojo Colorado, page 204, or other mojo sauce.

6 servings

A waiter at the Cervecería La Abadia in Granada was kind enough to tell me how this savory dish was made.

# *Repollo con Comino*

## Cabbage with Toasted Cumin

*1 teaspoon cumin seeds*
*2 tablespoons olive oil*
*1 small head green cabbage, shredded (about 4 cups)*
*1/4 cup water*
*2 teaspoons vinegar*
*1/2 teaspoon salt*

1. Toast cumin seeds in large skillet over medium-low heat for 3 to 4 minutes or until aromatic, stirring constantly.
2. Add oil to skillet; heat over medium heat until hot. Add cabbage; sauté several minutes. Add water; bring to a boil. Reduce heat to low; cover and steam about 5 minutes or until cabbage is just tender.
3. Stir in vinegar and salt. Serve at room temperature as a tapa or side dish.

4 to 6 servings

A delicious find, a whole new taste for cabbage, as I discovered at Las Cumbres, Taberna Andaluza, in Madrid.

Autora
Author

# *Torrijas*

## French Toast with Honey

2 eggs
1 cup whole milk
Olive oil for frying
4 (5/8-inch-thick) slices dense white bread
Honey
Cinnamon

1. In shallow pan, combine eggs and milk; beat well.
2. Generously cover bottom of large skillet with oil. Heat over medium heat until hot. Dip bread in egg mixture. Fry about 4 minutes on each side or until golden brown.
3. Place French toast on individual dessert plates. Generously drizzle with honey; sprinkle with cinnamon.

4 servings

As the barman at Cafe Cáceres in Sevilla said, 'You have to make it with love. Everything that's made with love turns out well.

# Tapa de Sardinas y Tomate

## Sardine and Tomato Tapa

8 (3/8-inch-thick) slices baguette
Extra virgin olive oil
2 tablespoons pine nuts
1 medium tomato, peeled, seeded and chopped*
Sardines

1. Heat broiler. Place baguette slices on cookie sheet. Drizzle each with oil. Broil until toasted.
2. Toast pine nuts in small skillet over medium-low heat for 3 to 5 minutes or until light golden brown, stirring occasionally. Cool; coarsely chop.
3. Combine pine nuts and tomato. Spread on toasted baguette slices. Top each with 1 or 2 sardines.
*See page 35.

8 tapas

The toasted pine nuts add unusual flavor and crunch. This is similar to a tapa I enjoyed at El Paradís Restaurant in Madrid.

Autora Author

# Anchoas con Olivas y Ajo

## Anchovies with Olives and Garlic

1 (2-oz.) jar or can rolled anchovy fillets
Assorted green olives
Thin slices garlic

1. Arrange anchovies and olives on small serving plate.
2. Sprinkle with garlic. Serve with toothpicks.

This couldn't be easier!

# Tapa de Otoño

## Cheese and Apple Butter Tapa

8 (3/8-inch-thick) slices baguette

8 slices cheese (such as Manchego or queso blanco)

8 teaspoons apple or pumpkin butter

8 whole walnuts

Top each baguette slice with 1 slice of cheese, 1 teaspoon apple butter and 1 walnut.

8 tapas

The original 'butter' was probably made with quince, but apple or pumpkin butter is a tasty alternative.

*Crema Catalana*

Back home, one hot night in July, I was
preparing Crema Catalana for guests. In Spain
I had purchased an electric flaming device
for the burnt sugar topping, but the little
transformer I had wouldn't even heat up the
coil. Fortunately, my cousin happened to call
and he told me about a similar experience
he'd had trying to get a samovar to work, and
where to find a higher-voltage transformer.
Now well prepared, but forgetful, I started
flaming only a half hour before our guests
were to arrive. Unfortunately, the hot night
with no breeze left our kitchen full of
smoke. The fire alarm began shrieking just as
the guests arrived, one holding a huge bunch
of gladiolas in her arms. I raced to the
phone, alerted the alarm service, all seemed
under control. Back in the kitchen we were
watching the final flames (my friend, glads
still in her arms, looked like a beautiful
statue), and then ... sirens! The fireman had
come anyway 'We always go just to make sure.'
It seemed like a lot of tax dollars to spend
on a pudding, but it was delicious.

*Judy and Emily*

*Rusty and Audrey*

My thanks go to a team of extraordinary artists and culinary professionals who helped shape this book: Emily Oberg, cookbook designer par excellence, and creator of hundreds of beautiful table settings; Audrey Nelson, whose talent and expertise helped shape the majority of the recipes; her husband and sous chef, Rusty Nelson, who kept us laughing as well as on target; Judy Tills, who worked on recipe development until time wouldn't permit; Jim Oberg who set up lighting when winter sent us indoors; and Susan Kroese who first understood my dream. Thanks to my poetry group—Lois Berg, Sarah Orman and Deb Prazak, and to my brother, Amos Deinard, for keeping an eye on my words; and to Rosa Rull for watching over my Spanish. On the wrap-up end, I thank Nancy Lilleberg, a super recipe editor, Leslie Hacking who brilliantly made all the pieces come together as one, despite frequent trips to local bistros in search of oxtails, and Bruce Pettit who managed the final production.

Over the months, I tested all the recipes and usually found people willing to taste and give their honest opinons, some of which came out downright poetic. I thank them all.

Most of all, I want to thank my husband, Erwin, who has championed me every step of the way, and personally sampled almost 200 dishes. And to our children: Robert, who helped me with recipe naming, found more textual errors than I thought possible, and was a super tasting organizer, bringing together great groups of friends; Sarah, who brought her professorial skills to editing my text; and Peter, once a professional cook, who taught me many a kitchen trick, starting with how to use a French chef's knife. They have always inspired me and been at my side with support, prodding me from time to time to move me into the next century or at least new technologies. They are all great cooks!

These are approximate, rounded measures.

**Weight**
1 ounce = 28 grams
4 ounces = 114 grams
8 ounces (1/2 pound) = 225 grams
16 ounces (1 pound) = 450 grams
32 ounces (2 pounds) = 900 grams
36 ounces (2-1/4 pounds) = 1 kilogram

**Quantity**
1/4 teapsoon = 1.25 ml
1/2 teaspoon = 2.5 ml
1 teaspoon = 5 ml
1 tablespoons (3 teaspoons) = 15 ml
1/4 cup (4 tablespoons) = 60 ml
1/3 cup (5-1/3 tablespoons) = 79 ml
1/2 cup (8 tablespoons) = 118 ml
1 cup = 237 ml
2 cups (1 pint) = 480 ml
2 pints (1 quart) = 950 ml
4 quarts (1 gallon) = 375 liters

**Oven temperatures**
300°F = 150°C
325°F = 160°C
350°F = 175°C
375°F = 190°C
400°F = 200°C
425°F = 220°C
450°F = 230°C

**Length**
1/2 inch = 1.25 cm
1 inch = 2.5 cm
8 inches = 20 cm
10 inches = 25 cm

**All-purpose flour**
1/3 cup (1.5 oz) = 42 gm
1/2 cup (2.2 oz) = 63 gm
1 cup (4.4 oz) = 125 gm.

**Granulated sugar**
1 tablespoon (.4 oz) = 12 gm
1/4 cup (1.8 oz) = 50 gm
1/3 cup (24 oz) = 67 gm
1/2 cup (3.5 oz) = 100 gm
1 cup (7.1 oz) = 200 gm

*Spanish sherry from Andalucía*

More and more Spanish products are becoming available in local supermarkets, from Manchego, Idiazabal and Mahon cheeses, to piquillo peppers, pimentón (paprika), and azafrán (saffron). There are also some excellent web sites that specialize in Spanish foods, cookbooks and cookware.

For the most complete offering of Spanish cookware, such as paella pans and earthenware cazuelas; for cookbooks; and for foods that will make you hungry just reading about them—teas, nuts, legumes, olives, olive oil, guindilla peppers, dried ñora peppers, pimentón, preserved fish and shellfish, squid ink, seasonings, rice, sauces, turrón and much more, the place to shop is The Spanish Table:
www.tablespan.com
Pike Street Hillclimb
1427 Western Ave.
Seattle, WA 98101
Phone: 206-682-2827
Fax: 206-682-2814

*Fruit and vegetable market, Granada*

Also offering incredible variety in cookbooks, cookware, tile, and foods—capers, cheeses, chorizo, fruits and nuts, serrano ham, olive oil, olives, piquillo peppers, rice, turrón and more, contact Tienda.com:
www.tienda.com
Phone: 888-472-1022
Catalog available

Another site of interest, again with cookware, gas burners, paella pans, and gourmet foods such as charcuterie, sweets, fish, paella rice, Navarra asparagus, saffron, etc. is La Española Meats:
www.laespanolameats.com
25020 Doble Ave.
Harbor City, CA
310-539-0455

For pimentón, olive oils and vinegars, another site worth checking is Rogers International LTD:
www.RogersIntl.com
94 Neal Street
Portland, ME 04102
Phone: 207-879-2641

For olive oils and vinegars, including sherry, Chardonnay and cava vinegar; and cheeses such as Manchego, Mahon, Queso de Vare, and Picón, contact Zingerman's:
www.zingermans.com
620 Phoenix Drive
Ann Arbor, MI 48108
To receive a catalog, call: 888-636-8162

For spices of all kinds, a wonderful place is Penzeys Spices:
www.penzeys.com
Phone: 800-741-7787
Fax: 262-679-7878
Catalog available

In the U.S. we don't usually follow the classic Spanish order of first course, second course, dessert; except, perhaps, in restaurants. What in Spain is considered a first course, including eggs, bean dishes, pastas and seafood salads, might make a light meal or a main course here. Vegetable dishes are often eaten separately as a first course as well. Our main meal is customarily at night; in Spain it's at late midday. But, these dishes are meant to be enjoyed when and how you will, and in any combination. Some recipes, at least to their creators, will appear more "adapted" than exact, but cooking is always a work in progress.

*Nuria Jiménez Uroz*

*"Dinner, at night? Each house is another world. At my house, dinner at night hardly exists. It's a very informal meal. Here the main meal is in the afternoon. Dinner at home could be a salad, or a French omelet, or not much at all.*

Menu of the day, Barcelona

*The midday meal usually has a first course, a second course and a dessert. It depends on the place, but the first course can be a salad, or vegetables, or heartier dishes. At home it's typically a salad, or something more filling like potaje (stew). And for the second course, well, meat, or chicken, or fish. First and second courses are not about size. They're different types of food.*

*Here we eat tapas as an evening meal. But, if you go to the north of Spain or the south of Spain, it's the reverse. They go out for tapas and afterward they go out and eat two courses.*

*'Traditional cooking' depends on the region. In the cities, it's done less and less because traditional cooking is very elaborate. When you don't have time to cook, you eat faster and more simply. I suppose it also depends on what you're used to eating."*

245

*The boyfriend*

*Specialties of Olot, Catalunya*

*Empanadas, breads: Market, Santiago de Compostela*

*Parc Güell, Barcelona*

# Bibliography

## General information sites on the internet include:

http://www.andalucia.org/spa/rutas/rgastro.htm (Andalucía)

http://www.galinor.es (Galicia)

http://www.upv.es/cv/valgastr.html (Valencia)

http://www.red2000.com/spain/1gastro/html (all regions)

http://www.visitaeuskadi.com (País Vasco)

Generalitat de Catalunya, KPPT0010@correu.gencat.es (Catalunya)

## Books:

Aris, Pepita. *The Spanishwoman's Kitchen*. London: The Orion Publishing Group, 1999.

Aris, Pepita. *Recipes from a Spanish Village*. London: Conran Octopus Limited, 1993.

Casas, Penelope. *¡Delicioso! The Regional Cooking of Spain*. New York: Alfred A. Knopf, 1999.

Casas, Penelope. *The Foods & Wines of Spain*. New York: Alfred A. Knopf, 2000.

Davenport, Forsyth, Noble, Nollen, Simonis. *Spain*. Melbourne: Lonely Planet Publications, 1997.

Garcia, Clarita. *Clarita's Cocina: Great Traditional Recipes from a Spanish Kitchen*. Tampa: Surfside Publishing, 1990.

Herbst, Sharon Tyler. *Food Lover's Companion*. New York: Barron's Educational Series, Inc., 1990.

Marrodán Prados, Igone. *Madrid al Fuego*. Madrid: Sílex, D.L. 1999.

Ortiz, Elisabeth Lambert. *The Food of Spain and Portugal: The Complete Iberian Cuisine*. New York: Atheneum, 1989.

Ostmann, Barbara Gibbs and Baker, Jane L. *The Recipe Writer's Handbook*. New York: John Wiley & Sons, Inc., 2001.

Trutter, Marion, ed. *Culinaria Spain*. Cologne: Culinaria Könemann, 1998.

## Booklets:

*Azafrán Natural Artesano*. Azafrán Natural, S.L., C/Rio Mesa, Barbarela 11, No. 16, 2/A2, 29620 Torremolinos, Málaga, España

*Barcelona; Lleida; Costa Daurada; and Costa Brava*. Turespaña, Ministerio de Economia y Hacienda, Secretaria de Estado de Comercio, Turismo y PYMES.

*Castilla y León. Gastronomía*. Castilla y León Información Turística, c/Calixto Fernández de la Torre, 6; 47001 Valladolid.

*Galicia Terra Unica. El viaje esperado*. Turgalicia, Dirección Xeral de Turismo

*Gastronomía Andaluza*. Guías Prácticas; Viajes y Cultura; Junta de Andalucía

*Gastronomia. Comunidad Valenciana*. Agencia Valenciana del Turisme; Paz, 48; 46003 Valencia.

*Gastronomy - The Basque Country*. Eusko Jaurlaritza; Merkataritza, Kontsumo, eta Turismo Saila; 2nd Edition, January, 1993.

*Gobierno Vasco*. Departamento de Comercio, Consumo y Turismo; 2nd Edition, January, 1993.

*Junta de Castilla y León*. Pza. Mayor, 10; 40001 Segovia

*Los Autenticos Sabores del Queso Español*. Consorcio de los Quesos Tradicionales de España, S.A.

*Madrid Gastronomia. Colección Arte y Costumbres de Madrid*. Dirección General de Turismo, Consejería de Economía y Empleo, Comunidad de Madrid.

*Nuestra Cocina. La Gallega*. Asociación Gallega de Cocineros.

Otero, Gloria. *Spanish Cooking*. Turespaña, Secretaria de Estado de Comercio, Turismo y PYME. Ministerio de Economia y Hacienda.

*Spain*. Turespaña, Secretaria de Estado de Comercio, Turismo y PYME. Ministerio de Economía y Hacienda.

*Tenerife*. Turespaña, Secretaría de Estado de Comercio, Turismo y PYME. Ministerio de Economía y Hacienda.

*Turespaña*. Ministerio de Economia y Hacienda, Secretaria de Estado de Comercio, Turismo y PYME; Junta de Castilla y León.

*Ycoden Daute Isora Denominación de Origen*. c/La Palmita, 10; 388440 La Guancha, Tenerife, Islas Canarias.

*View from the Alhambra. Granada*